THE LA NANNY
BOOK

The LA Nanny Book

A Book for Nannies and Parents

LARISSA NEILSON

Edited by Ivonne Arias

authorHOUSE®

AuthorHouse™ LLC
1663 Liberty Drive
Bloomington, IN 47403
www.authorhouse.com
Phone: 1-800-839-8640

Published by AuthorHouse   07/18/2013

ISBN: 978-1-4817-6819-1 (sc)
ISBN: 978-1-4817-6817-7 (hc)
ISBN: 978-1-4817-6818-4 (e)

Library of Congress Control Number: 2013911471

Cover Photo by: David Vigliotti
Little Learners Lodge- Parent and Teaching Community
www.mmpschool.com

CONTENTS

"You don't write because you want to say something, you write because you have something to say"

—F Scott Fitzgerald

Faith fuels my endeavors. To God for giving me the gift of writing, to my daughter Esther, who is my strength and joy and to all the children I was lucky to share my life with throughout these years.

ACKNOWLEDGEMENTS

I want to thank my parents for their love and support, my daughter for her patience during this journey, my inspiring pastors Richard and Fonda Hays, my amazing editor Ivonne Arias whose help was crucial in writing this book.

To Magda Gerber for her wisdom, insights and hard work in introducing Dr. Emmi Pikler's unconventional approach to the United States.

INTRODUCTION

When I thought about writing this book, I first wanted to search into my motives for doing it. I thought about all my beliefs: to help, to serve, to give back to my community, and what has helped me that others can find useful. I've learned so much about the nanny world that I feel it's time to share these insights. I thought about all those nannies I met throughout the years with some kind of issue at work, struggling with the children they cared for. I remember the many questions they had, and the phrases repeated to me over and over, "Oh, I didn't know that," or "If I only knew that!"

This book is an effort to narrate what it takes to be a full-time nanny in LA. I picked LA because I've lived and worked as a nanny here for over a decade. Although I don't know what it's like to be a nanny in Montana or New York, some of the issues I address in this book, nanny-wise, may be considered general. This book is intended for people who have chosen or are thinking about the nanny career as a permanent job. If you're only working as a nanny or baby sitter because your "dream job" hasn't knocked on your door yet, this book may not be for you.

Whether you're considering working in the childcare industry in a private home or a childcare center, or you are a child care provider, parent, or nanny, you'll find useful tools and advice that will help you understand the subject and achieve your goals.

While doing some research for this book, I was surprised to find out that most information about the subject was for parents looking for a nanny. Several websites advise, warn, and inform new families about what to do when hiring a nanny, from how much to pay and what to do if things get out of hand. Some nanny agency websites feature videos teaching aspiring nannies how to dress and what to say.

I also found some suggestions like a nanny evolving into a "nanny manager," meaning that if you were the long-standing nanny for a family and the kids are now going to school, you become a sort of family assistant; running the errands, going to the bank, grocery shopping etc. After seeing all of these things, I knew I had to write this book and without being judgmental, I don't think someone who enjoys and knows the importance of his/her job as a nanny would exchange the chance to help a new family for the chance to become a "nanny manager." The job of a caretaker has a great impact on children's lives. It's a job that should never be overlooked or denied the importance it deserves. Throughout the next pages, you'll see why. It is my hope to raise a new generation of nannies who are not only the well-intended caregivers, but also nanny educators.

This book will also give you information and instructions for working as a nanny. What gives me the word? Experience. Throughout the years I have learned the system, identified the most common issues when working as a nanny, and found the solution to them. I've worked in the childcare business in the greater Los Angeles area for over a decade now, helping and serving single and high-profile families (chef included) from Atwater Village all the way to Pacific Palisades.

I'm grateful I was blessed to share my life with wonderful families with lovely children. I still keep in touch with all of them, because in the end, it's service that counts, quality that lasts, and relationships that have eternal value. I'll share with you all my experiences and what I've learned with these families. It's been an exciting road for me. Being an LA nanny is amazing!

I feel fortunate for the opportunities given to me and I'm so grateful for each family that's enriched my life in many ways.

FOREWORD

RIE Parent-Infant Guidance® classes are usually just for parents and their babies but several years ago, I taught a class where a nanny regularly attended with a mother and her baby daughter. She would sit quietly and observe the babies, along with the rest of the group. I noticed how peaceful and calm she seemed to be, how slowly she moved and that her interactions with the baby she cared for were always respectful. That nanny was Larissa Neilson and I am pleased and honored to write the foreword to her book especially for nannies.

Larissa has always been an enthusiastic proponent of Magda Gerber's Educaring® Approach, which is the respectful approach to being with babies that we teach at RIE. Larissa has a passion for this approach and a deep and abiding care for babies and their families. She is a true professional, always looking for ways to improve the lives of the babies in her care. I suppose it was only a matter of time before all of this compelled Larissa to write a book and how lucky we are that she did!

The LA Nanny Book is one of just a few books written by a nanny, for nannies, or for someone considering a nanny career. It is comprehensive and includes all sorts of practical information—from resume writing and interviewing for a job to establishing harmonious relationships with employers and co-workers. I am especially pleased that Larissa has included several chapters about the Educaring® Approach.

Many of the nannies and professional caregivers who have studied this approach remark that following its principles has made their work easier and more enjoyable, and that they no longer go home exhausted at the end of the day. It has helped them to find answers to the inevitable challenges that arise when caring for babies and toddlers. I hope that as you read this book, you will see how the Educaring® Approach can help to make your work more easier and more enjoyable too.

Thank you, Larissa, for being an ambassador for RIE and for writing *The LA Nanny Book*. I believe it will be an invaluable resource for nannies everywhere and for anyone who cares for an infant or young child.

Deborah Carlisle Solomon
RIE Executive Director
www.rie.org
Author of *Baby Knows Best: Raising a Confident and Resourceful Child, the RIE Way*
May 2013

PART ONE

CHAPTER 1

CHOOSING TO BECOME A NANNY

I don't know where you stand right now while you read this book. Maybe you're a seasoned nanny with some or much experience in the field. Maybe you're someone who's just thinking about becoming one. Maybe you're someone who sometimes thinks about it because you like children. Or maybe you're a professional with a degree in child development who knows a lot about children and their world. No matter what your background is, you'll find useful tips and will be offered tools to achieve a fulfilling career as a nanny. I welcome you all and let me tell you how it all began for me.

I started to work as a nanny as soon as I got to Los Angeles, by chance, because I was visiting a friend who had a friend who needed some help with the children. Luckily for me, this lady would introduce me to a very interesting parenting philosophy called the Educaring® Approach. I'll share more about it in the second part of the book. Let me tell you that the knowledge of the Educaring® Approach was crucial for my career as a nanny. I have to recognize that the application of its principles took me to a degree that can beat any child development class. I read all the books about this approach, I took the children to the classes, and that's when I thought about taking on the nanny job as a profession because I understood how critical the role of a caretaker is in a child's growth and development.

It is my hope to defeat the thoughts of, "Oh, anyone can take care of children," or "Taking care of children is so easy, I have baby brothers I cared for," "I have raised my own children, so of course I can work as a nanny."

Let's look at some definitions. According to *Dictionary. com*, "A nanny is a person usually with special training employed to care for children in a household." Let's see how *Dictionary.com* defines a babysitter: someone employed "To take charge of a child while the parents are temporarily away."

Now let me give you my definition of a nanny after all these years: "A nanny is a professional childcare provider who works in a private home on a full-time basis providing quality care to infants and children. It is not a job; it is a valued profession. She plays a critical role in the child's growth and development. She educates while she cares, it is her goal to help raise a well-understood child and to develop a relationship with parents that has eternal value." I don't say "a happy child" because that's a cliché, and you'll understand that as you read this book.

There are many thoughts you can entertain while choosing to become a nanny in LA. It's well-paid, looks easy to do, and some good jobs can give you good benefits, like paid vacations, sick days, health insurance, and so on. But, how to get the good ones? Let me tell you that from small beginnings come great things.

I became a nanny kind of by accident and then while working, I understood something I believed in and embraced. I remember my first job paid me eight dollars per hour, and was Monday through Friday, 8:00 am to 5:00 pm, Saturdays to babysit, and occasional Sundays if the parents were to attend parties. Luckily, it was only one child. And yeah, I did light housekeeping, like passing the Swiffer across the hardwood floors (there was dog hair all the time), loading the dishwasher and then putting the dishes away, doing the family's laundry, some ironing (this was beyond belief!) and some cooking. Wow, I got tired just writing it down! But let me tell you, it paid off. This was the job that led me to *the* philosophy.

The lady of the house made sure I read all the books pertaining to the Educaring® Approach, took me to RIE® Parent-Infant Guidance classes, and gave me the chance to practice the principles with the baby. So while I was working hard, I was learning something that would completely change the way I saw and engaged children from then on. After almost two years of service, I had to go away. The family set a date for all of us to go to a nice place to have a good-bye dinner and in the end, this lady wrote such a great recommendation letter that not even me writing it on my own behalf would've come up with something *that* good. This letter opened up the doors to the next level.

So if you'd like to work as a nanny and you've already had this kind of entry level job, be glad that you're ready to move up to the next level. Now, this isn't the rule. You may start off with an awesome "take-care-of-the-baby-only job," but that doesn't happen all the time.

While working for this first family and going for walks or to the park, I met several nannies who complained about the "light housekeeping." They said that they were supposed to be nannies and not housekeepers. Let me tell you that this is an issue that can be solved before you begin to work; we will discuss that in Chapter 5. These nannies also complained that the children were good to them, but not when the parents were present. They would say that the parents don't discipline the children and that they were bad to them, yet another reason for them not to be happy at their workplace, let alone with the children.

How you respond to the job once you're there has to do a lot with your personality. For example, I'm a very calm person, quiet, soft spoken, and patient. That can help out when the child would hit me or would say to me, "I don't want to play with you," "I want you to go away." Very early in my career, I understood that I can never take a toddler's words personally because I'm a full-grown woman with an understanding of children's behaviors based on many situations. So how do you handle that? I'm not saying that if you're not calm, quiet, soft spoken, and patient, then you can't be a nanny; that can help, but what ultimately will determine your reaction and how to handle that situation, among others, is the way you see the child, the relationship you have built up with him, and your knowledge of the family's background before the situation comes up.

Throughout the years working as a nanny, I learned a lot about American families. No matter where they lived or what their background was, they all shared general common goals, dreams, fears, worries, trends, and they were all looking for someone to trust with the most valuable thing in their lives: their children. And most of these families were brand new parents trying to do their best at raising their children with a great deal of fear and excitement for the new. Can you see the enormous importance of having someone who can actually be of great help to those brand new parents? Here, stop and think about it! The role of the helper becomes of great importance!

And at some point, every family, mostly in LA, needs and hires a nanny to help with the baby. Once I started working as a nanny, I started learning from day one. My knowledge is experiential and came from sensitive observation of the child, which we will learn more about in Part Two.

Up to this point, you've learned a little about what it takes to work as a nanny. Now when thinking about becoming a nanny, you will find some specific qualifications required to work. Let's check out this ad:

> "Fantastic Nanny for a family. This position requires someone who has **at least 5 years of experience** as a nanny in a home with wonderful references. Nanny should speak English fluently and have good communication skills. Position calls for the care of twin almost 3-year-olds as well as a baby who is on the way soon!! **NEWBORN experience is a must**. Mom will be at home so nanny must be comfortable working alongside mom AND be confident working independently as well. Perfect fit will be someone who is loving and nurturing yet energetic and active as it is needed to keep up with the twins!! Education in Child Development is preferred. There will be light healthy cooking required for the children as well as errand running from time to time. Please have a reliable car and insurance. The nanny must be available and flexible to travel with the family on vacations. This position is for someone who can truly commit long-term. It is a

wonderful opportunity for a mature nanny with a
stellar background. This is a loving family who is
interested in a great match so please only reply if
you have the required background stated above.
Salary: D.O.E".

This position calls for a "seasoned" nanny. I choose it
randomly, because it has a newborn infant and toddlers.
When I started to work, I began with only one baby, in order
to learn. As I've mentioned, I was lucky I landed in a home
where the lady was a first-time mom and she was applying
very interesting principles to raising her son.

As you see, this job demands at least five years of
experience and someone who can handle three children
at once; but even when I have the experience required, I
wouldn't take this job because for me, that's too much and
knowing what I know can be stressing and highly demanding.
A newborn requires a lot of observation time to understand
the baby's cues, signs, likes, and dislikes. Everything is brand
new to the baby; the light, the noise, too cold, too hot. The
baby requires "sensitive observation." On the other hand, the
twins are toddlers who are discovering their autonomy and
constantly pushing the limits of what they can and cannot
do. They probably attend classes and have their own world
and require a lot of attention and observation in order to get
to know them and build the relationship. Maybe they're just
moving up after their previous caretaker. It's helpful to find
out who was before you and so forth.

But if I had the chance to be with this family from the
beginning when the twins were born, I would stay with them.
Why? Because I helped raise them. By the time those twins
reach three years old, my job is completely done! They would

probably have a set schedule for meals, snacks, and classes and would most likely be able to understand words because they're used to having everything that happens to them explained to them before it happens. By the time the new baby arrives, they were probably given an explanation and told about what to expect when their baby brother or sister arrives. I hope you can see the difference.

One thing some people have criticized me about is that I'll never start a job with a toddler. I have to mention that all these years, I always started with two-month-old babies. Without knowing, I became an infant care specialist; ever since I learned the Educaring® Approach, I embraced it as my own and when moving on from families I'll always choose a newborn. There are professionals who care for newborns until they are two months old, such as nurses, doulas, grandmas, etc. People tend to think, "Oh, of course a newborn only sleeps!" While it's mostly true, it's not the rule. One of the babies I cared for since he was two months old used to sleep for 45 minutes and then be awake for four hours straight! And then he would go for another 45 minutes of napping. Later on, we'll learn that a good nap is a two-hour one. You'll see how important it is for children to sleep. See the "Resources" section for more information.

If you're at the start of your career as a nanny, choose a family with only one child as your first job in order to learn and gain experience. You'll learn here that the nanny job doesn't consist of getting to work to "entertain" the child, feed him change diapers, and keep him from falling; it goes beyond. You can be teaching, educating the parents and the child while you care!

Let's look at some facts about childcare that every person who intends to work as a nanny should know:

- The first years of life are crucial for intellectual, social and general development—80 percent of the brain develops by age 3 and nearly 90 percent by the age of 5 (Reef 2012).
- Children who experience higher quality child care consistently show somewhat better cognitive function and language development across the first three years of life. Higher quality child care also predicts greater school readiness at four and a half years of age. ("Child Care Industry" 2012)
- A study of interactions concluded that the words spoken by primary caregivers to children in their early years account for 59 percent of the cognitive accomplishments of preschool-age children. ("Child Care Industry" 2012)
- Well-designed pre-k programs are part of the solution to school success. But, children aren't born at age 4 and given the hours that children spend in child care, it can no longer be ignored as an early learning setting. (Reef 2012)

I hope you can see the importance of your work as a nanny. This book aims to encourage nannies to start working with new families with their first born children, since I believe the first five years of life are crucial for their future. I do respect all the nannies who love and enjoy taking care of toddlers and older children, but my focus is the early years.

And if you're thinking about being a nanny only until you get a "better" or the "ideal" job, or because the economic situation demands you to work, you won't be really committed to the job let alone to the child, and you won't be satisfied with yourself either. This is about the life of a brand new human being!

CHAPTER 2

How to Start? When? Where?

Regardless of your educational background or your previous work experience, think about all the things you've done throughout your life to this day that you believe will be helpful with caring for children. We always learn something about children. It can be in our own families when growing up, or through school and later through our relationships with friends. As I mentioned before, all my knowledge of child development is experiential, learned through practice and the study of the Educaring® Approach, I'll tell you about it later on; but if I were to start it all over again from zero, I'd definitely go ahead and take child development classes about raising children wherever they are provided; parenting groups, etc. Times have changed and we can no longer provide care for our children based on the past. We love and appreciate our mothers' and grandmothers' teachings, but these times are different than theirs.

Now if you've already worked as a nanny, great, because it's time to build up a résumé. Yes, nannies need a résumé where you can list your educational background and work experience. Remember that how you present your résumé says a lot about yourself.

While working on my résumé, besides the heading with my name, objective, education, certification (First Aid, CPR, etc), work experience, skills and abilities, I decide to add on "Personal Statement," "Childcare Service Philosophy," and "Hobbies and Interests" sections. You'll be seen the way you see yourself, so the personal statement is the "you" besides your name and education. A Childcare Service Philosophy is you saying, "I won't only change diapers and care for your child, but I also have the knowledge of this philosophy that works when engaging children." We'll discuss the philosophy in the second part of the book. And finally, I add on the visuals. I made a book, like a scrapbook you'd make when getting married, where you collect every single detail. I put pictures of the babies I cared for, letters, and thank you cards from the families and children I served. I decorated with every baby's special characteristics or the baby's first word, and some famous quotes about children. The result was amazing; seeing a book of beautiful, smiling babies and you next to them says a lot about you. Last but not least, it's always a good idea to create your business cards and some flyers to drop off whenever necessary.

After you've prepared all of the above, you're ready to go out and look for a job. I'd start letting everyone around you know about your search. Who knows, someone may know somebody who needs help with their children; remember, that's how I began. Then, go to local places where classes for children are held and ask for permission to drop a flyer or stick it on their board. There are lots of online parenting groups and resources for new parents where you can also post your ad. There's Craigslist, which I was once hired through by the way. Then we have domestic agencies that will start the search for you once you fill out an application. Here in LA, there are many domestic agencies, depending on the area you live in. A good start when looking for a job is to first choose the areas you can work. For example if you live in the Valley, you may not want to go to places on the Westside, such as Malibu, Santa Monica, Pacific Palisades, etc., unless of course you're single and have availability. This is a very important piece of advice because some agencies will send you wherever in order to send as many candidates as possible to jobs. You need to be clear about this.

Another thing I want to point out is that if you visit a nanny agency and you have to pay a fee for the application, walk away. Nanny agencies in LA charge 15-20% of your annual income to the family that hires you, which is a lot of money, so they shouldn't charge you to fill out an application. Here you will have to present proof of eligibility to work in the USA, your social security number, and an application, which is sometimes ten pages long. Besides that, you'll drop off a copy of your wonderful résumé and you'll be asked for recommendation letters if any, and telephone numbers of the families you worked for. There will be a background and driving record check, and the agency will call your references before sending you to interviews.

When filling out the application, be specific, yet flexible. If you're a single person, you're a candidate for 50 to 60 hours of work through the week and can be open for travel. But if you're married or single with children, be specific about the areas you want to work in, considering if you need to be back home at a certain time of day, and the hours, days and traveling. It seems like pretty much common sense, but sometimes the first issues come from not clarifying times and days.

After you're sure about the hours you're willing to commit, financial topics should be covered, such as your hourly rate or the salary you're willing to accept based on hours. The hourly rate varies depending on years of experience, recommendation letters, driving record, educational background, and so forth, but it doesn't end there. You'll also have to say that there are six holidays that you won't work and you expect to be paid for: New Year's Day, Memorial Day, Independence Day (4th of July), Labor Day, Thanksgiving Day, and Christmas Day. Make sure to also specify that you'd like to be paid on the books, and any other specific requirement you may think of. In my case, I won't work Sundays at all. Think about your lifestyle and say this from the very beginning so you don't have to say it later. All these processes may take you half a day. At the end in the "Resources" section of the book, you'll find a small list of places where children's classes are held, websites that allow you to post your ad.

To finish up with domestic agencies, I have to tell you that in LA, visiting a Westside agency can be disappointing. I know some agencies that won't take you seriously if you're not the blonde, blue-eyed American nanny, or if you don't have traveling experience or a European type of car, even if it's old. They might allow you to fill out the application, but would never call you. All these times, I wondered what all that has to do with the skills to help raise a child. I'm a Hispanic brunette gal and I know what I'm talking about. Supposedly, those agencies are to provide for the Hollywood stars and very high-profile nannies. As I write this book, I'm working for a big Hollywood star and I didn't get this job through an agency, so don't get discouraged. Remember, work faithfully and with a good heart. Your first jobs will be your way to the big ones because in the end, what gets you to this kind of job is your experience and what people have to say about your work.

CHAPTER 3

JOB SEEKING AND THE INTERVIEW PROCESS

Once you're sent to interview with prospective families, the game is on! While there are many tips to nail an interview, I just say be yourself; dress clean and conservative, don't wear perfume, and take notes during the interview because you will for sure have questions regarding schedules, days, travel flexibility, etc.

I remember during my very first interview, when asked what would be the most important quality for taking care of a child, I said "love." To this day, I wonder what the lady thought of that; she just looked at me and smiled. I can't remember what other questions were asked, but I remember she was very clear about the schedules and days. I've gone through interviews where the parents expected me to do the talking, and I've been in others where the parents sat me in a chair with a big light over my head and asked the unthinkable: what would you do if there's an earthquake? What would you do if you are with the child on a rainy day and got yourselves locked out and you don't have a cell phone or an umbrella? What do you do if you are at the park and you realized you left the car keys inside the car, have no diaper bag, it's 90 degrees, and the baby has a poop? What would you do when a child throws herself on the floor and throws a fit at the grocery store? Some questions were tricky, like what do you do to discipline a child? Do you believe in time out? And so on.

I call them "tricky" because discipline is up to the parents. They're the ones who are to set up the rules. Today's parents rely so much on nannies to be the ones who discipline the children because they don't want to be the "bad guy." They work a lot during the day and when they come home or it's their time to be with the children, they don't want to upset the children and don't know how to say "no" or just set limits or rules. We'll learn about all that when discussing the Educaring® Approach. Plus, here in LA, talking about parenting means that parents here are definitely following a philosophy or a style, which in LA is so trendy! LA parenting is talking about blogs, magazines, plans, programs, green, eco, yoga, vegetarianism, veganism, you name it. Everywhere you look, there's a family doing something new and different when raising their children. Be aware of all this and be informed.

The last interview I had was a while ago. After so many interviews and many mistakes, I've pretty much learned how to manage them. Some interviews are with the parents only, and others have the child present. I like the second option because it gives you the chance to see if they have any parenting style or how they approach their child. It also gives you the chance to demonstrate how you'd approach the child. At any rate, it's better to start off talking with the parents and then ask them to bring the child.

In the beginning, they have a word. They would mainly talk about the qualities they're looking for in the candidates' schedules and character. They may describe the mechanics of the household: when they work and how long, or they may be working from home and be present all the time; also, what they expect you to do besides caring for the child, such as light cleaning, the child's laundry, scheduling the child's activities, driving the child to classes, play dates, school, and in some cases doing the grocery shopping. Traveling with the family also is a possibility. Be aware, some parents are new when interviewing candidates, so make sure you discuss all of the above if they don't.

Let's go over some common scenarios during an interview. Brand new parents with a newborn: This is a brand new family and most likely all their parenting knowledge started when the mother became pregnant, by reading books, from labor and nursing classes, and information about baby nurses and doulas, etc. Typically, the families start looking for a nanny when the baby is between two and four months, when the mom has decided to go back to work or start working from home. They are also inexperienced when interviewing. It's very important to always listen carefully to everything they have to say about what they're looking for. There will be families for which the most important thing is the schedule or long-term commitment, flexibility, experience with newborns, what you'd do while the baby sleeps, or what else you could do besides taking care of the baby, like cleaning and cooking for the baby. All these are most commonly discussed during an interview. I don't have experience working as a "live-in nanny" and have never gone to that kind of interview, but I guess the main thing I'd discuss would be the schedule.

This is how I would approach an interview with brand new parents with a newborn: I'd first tell them the hours I'm willing to commit and the days. I'll explain to the parents that I won't be there to "entertain" the child, but to support healthy growth and development, that I would treat her with respect for the whole human being she is and never like an object throughout all caring activities, including feeding, diapering, bathing, and sleeping. I would always explain everything I do unto her before doing it. I would slow down when engaging with her. I would learn cues and needs by observing. I would say that I'm patient and can stand crying not because I'm trained to, but because I learned that crying is not to be feared or suppressed; crying is to be acknowledged and listened to, because children are so brand new that anything can be a factor of crying besides hunger and tiredness, such as feeling too cold, too hot, too bright or just simply needing to be held and supported at the time. Sidonie Greenburg says it right, "Just as the smiles and gurgles and small sounds of satisfaction are infant language, crying is too" (Gerber 2000).

I would explain that I will establish a schedule based on the child's routine for everyday caring activities. I would explain that sleep for infants and children is of vital importance to their growth, only during a deep sleep will the body release the growth hormone. In *Healthy Sleep Habits, Happy Child,* Dr. Marc Weissbluth suggests a nap is not a 'real' nap if less than 45 minutes (Weissbluth 1999). My goal will be to develop good sleeping habits.

And as for additional help, I would commit to keep the child's play area and room tidy and do the child's laundry, and when the time comes for the child to have solid meals, if the child doesn't already eat solid foods, I would commit to some home cooking for the child. I won't commit to do any cleaning, since mostly all the families have a housekeeper once or twice a week. I'll explain the reasoning for my commitments later.

It's very important that you let the parents know you're a nanny and not a housekeeper. You either do one thing right or two half-way. Let them know that the child is the priority for you, and that you don't want to be too tired around the child. Newborns are sponges that can easily pick up the adult's energy. Don't commit to working more than eight hours a day, if you can, not only for your sake, but for the baby's. After such a long time with you, she needs mama and a couple of fresh hands. In order to build up a healthy relationship, all parties must be in harmony. This approach has been the general rule for me, since I usually start with newborns.

Now let's see when a toddler is around a young baby. Depending on the toddler's age, if two or older, I'll ask what kind of activities she's doing in the house and outside the house. If she goes to school, how many days per week? What's her relationship with the new baby like? What are the parents currently doing? Is there any particular parenting style they follow? I'd also ask if I would be caring mostly for the toddler or the youngest baby. I'd find out if they had a previous nanny; if yes, I'd ask the reasons why she left. Knowing all this will give you an idea of what the work will be like and help you decide better if you can or cannot commit to do it. And again, it's important to listen to the parents first before you talk.

When meeting babies, like in the first case with only the newborn, usually the mom is holding her and showing her to you. If they want you to hold the baby, first ask them where you could wash your hands before and when about to hold the baby, talk to the baby and introduce yourself. Wait and let the baby know you're about to hold her. This is what I meant when I wrote that I would always explain to the child everything I do unto her before doing it and not treat her as a passing object from hand to hand. This has such a great impact on the parents; they'll see how gentle and polite you are, not because you want to get the job, but because there are very good reasons to do it that will have a great impact on the baby's life and relationship with you. We'll also discuss this later.

When meeting a toddler, greet her and talk to her as you'd introduce yourself to another adult. Respect means that you won't say, "Oh, look how cute you are," or do any baby talking if for instance the child is just learning how to talk. Think about it. When you meet people, you wouldn't just go ahead and call them "cute" to their faces, so why we would do it to a child? Because she's smaller than us? Be observant of what she's doing or holding so you can establish a small talk, maybe you can say "I see you're holding a dinosaur," or "Do you like dancing?" if the child wiggles while standing there. These are only examples, my advice is be observant. Don't make an effort to get the child to like you; be natural and yourself. While interviewing, look around you so you can see if the house is child-proofed. Visit the child's room and if it's not, talk about the importance of creating a safe environment for the child. We'll see the importance of this later.

In this book, I'll cover nanny experiences from newborns to five-year-old toddlers. I have no experience with older children. Generally, children begin school at three and are no longer at home, although some families here in LA have nannies until the children finish elementary school. I assume the nanny basically helps with pick-ups from school, homework, and house errands at that age.

After this interview, you will for sure have an idea of what the work would be like, and if you believe they're the family you'd like to help, offer a trial day so you can have a better picture of the family and the child. If you follow these simple but common sense rules, you'll most likely have three to four families that liked you and are ready for the trial day. Here's where you take your notes out and go through all of them, and if you liked some of the families, you're up for a trial day!

CHAPTER 4

TRIAL DAY

A trial day should be set to start at the hours of work required by the job. If they need a nanny from 9 am to 5 pm, you need to start at 9 am. It's preferable to do it for the eight hours so you can have an idea of what the work will be like. While eight hours are ideal, sometimes new families with both parents working may demand schedules from 6 am until 7 pm. I'd work these hours if it's my first ever job as an entry-level nanny to learn and gain experience.

A few days before the trial day, get directions to the house, check traffic, and I'd even say drive by the house if you think you could get lost; sometimes not even GPS is accurate. You don't want to be late. Punctuality is key to me, not only for the trial day but from day one until the end. It says a lot about your responsibility, commitment and professionalism. We'll discuss this in-depth in the chapter about work ethics.

On that day, dress comfortable, don't wear perfume, and have your hair tied back especially if this trial day is for a baby between two and ten months old. Think about it, you'll most likely be holding the baby and while engaging the baby, your hair can't be in the way. Bring a small notebook to take notes of what you see and ask the parents if the child has a set schedule or daily routine or if they are about to set one up. You need to write all of this down. Ask casually, not with pressure; remember, it's only a trial day.

Let's picture the day now. Imagine you're on a trial day for an infant: so here you are, ringing the doorbell, parents open the door, and you are yourself, soft spoken and polite. We don't know if the baby is sleeping. If they're holding the baby, you greet each one of them. You walk in and parents take you to the baby's room or playing area. Many actions can happen here, but the main thing you're looking for is a safe playing area for you to be with the baby. At this point, you'll know if the house has been baby-proofed or not. If not, you need to point this out and explain the importance of having a safe environment for you and the baby to be in, as you'll see in the second part of the book.

After that, you'll most likely have some alone time with the baby. If the baby seems relaxed and content, find a spot and lay the baby down on his back and just sit next to him and observe. Don't try to entertain the baby; just let yourself watch what he's up to at this stage. If he is four months and up, he might be able to move some. Find the simplest toys of soft textures and place them close to him. Don't hand them to him or try to make the baby hold the toy. If the baby's interested enough he'll look for it and try to reach for it by himself, and keep on observing. There are good reasons to let the child be the initiator of what he wants to do. Talk to him gently, but as if you were talking to another adult; no baby talk allowed. Hopefully, the baby will be content for a good ten minutes at least. If he's not used to being on his back and starts to fuss, calmly narrate what you observe by saying, "I see you're getting upset from being on your back. I'll pick you up," and do it. Afterwards, you'll have a chance to explain to the parents everything you've observed.

When it's time for the baby to nurse or to be fed, you'll most likely be sitting next to the mom while she nurses or she may even give you the bottle to feed him. In the first case, if the mom starts talking to you while she's nursing, talk to her briefly and don't establish a conversation. After she's finished, explain to the mom the importance of giving the baby her full attention while nursing. You can read about nursing in the "Resources" section. In case you're given a bottle to feed the child, before you do it, explain gently and briefly to the baby that you'll do it. Say something like, "Owen I'll feed you with a bottle now. I know mommy or daddy always does it, but I'll help you today." Feed the bottle and be observant, try to keep eye contact with the baby, without forcing it until he finishes the bottle. Don't talk to anyone else while you're feeding and when he's done, say, "You finished the bottle." This is important because you establish a connection with the baby and he'll feel acknowledged and soothed.

When diapering time comes, again the same simple basic rules. Hopefully, there will be a place designated to do the diaper change. Here, you again say, "Owen you have a wet diaper and I'd like to change you." The changing of a diaper also deserves care and full attention because this is the time where the child refuels or reconnects. In the chapter about the Educaring® Approach, we'll go over changing diapers in detail, but I will say here that throughout the whole activity in a gentle manner and voice, you talk to the baby, narrating every step of the way. "I'm going to lay you down. I'm removing your diaper now. I see you peed. I see you have a poop. I'm going to wipe your bottom now. The cloth might feel cold on your skin. Thank you for letting me wipe you. I have a clean diaper to put on now. I'm going to attach the velcro now. I'll put your pants back on now." This is what I meant by not treating a baby as an object but as a whole human being that deserves all the respect of a whole human. This builds up an amazing trust between you and the baby. It builds up a connection; the baby understands and feels you and will feel comfortable with you. This applies to all ages.

Second scenario: a trial day for a six-month to one-year-old. Here, you'll start looking for a safe environment for the child. In this case, hopefully there will be a designated area for the child to play since at this age, they're more mobile and start crawling. Again, ask the parents for any established routines and so on. While having alone time with the child, don't try to entertain. Be observant and just place some toys around the child for him to pick up, and just have small talks, like, "I see you have several balls," "I wonder what you'd like to play with today." If the child isn't able to sit by himself yet, don't sit him up. Laying the child on his back is preferable, as explained in the Educaring® Approach chapter along with "uninterrupted playing."

When it's time for the child to eat, stick to the same rules as above. If you're invited to feed him, explain it to the child and do it. Hopefully, there aren't a lot of distractions surrounding the table or meal time, since children get easily distracted, so he can concentrate on the food. Don't forget to be observant. If the child shows you that he's enjoying the food say so, "I see you like the banana." During diapering time, the same rules apply. Try to get the child's attention, since at this point the child might be used to being offered a toy to "distract" him from the diapering time. After you've narrated every step of the way, the child will eventually enjoy diaper changes.

Since it's only one day, try to observe as much as you can and at the end, talk and present your observations to the parents about what you've learned from the child and how you'll be of help to him. And when saying goodbye, go to the child and say bye to him as well. People tend to forget about the child all the time. It's also a good idea to email the parents to say thank you and maybe share some ideas. This family will see that you are very different than the other candidates, and I assure you you'll get the job.

CHAPTER 5

ONCE YOU ARE HIRED

This moment may happen by the end of the trial day. It happened to me and it can happen to you. People will like you right away if you follow the simple common sense ideas I described in the chapter before. If this happens, one of the parents will come to talk to you and tell you. Here's your chance to say thank you very much and go over details, like the schedule. You want to be certain about it because you also have a life and it's good to know your schedule for sure, Monday through Thursday, or Tuesday through Saturday, or the classic Monday through Friday.

Say it, ask for it, and offer only the flexibility you're willing to commit. For example, at my last job, I said I could only work four days and nine hours per day. I won't work Sundays and I won't travel. However, after a year of having a wonderful relationship with the family, I actually ended up traveling and worked one Sunday and that's ok. The important thing here is for you to set a schedule that can't be changed unless it's good for you. Other than that, talk about the six holidays you won't work, and specify that if you do work those holidays, you'd need to get paid double the rate. Ask about your vacations, how many days or weeks. Ask about sick days, let them know that you expect to be paid for both and of course, set your hourly rate.

You can also be offered a salary. I'd actually rather get paid hourly because I have control of how many hours. With a salary, no matter how few or many hours you work, you get paid the same money. In practice, it's most common for you to find that you worked the most hours. That's up to you.

State that you will need to get paid for the 52 working weeks of the year, and whenever the family is out of town, for any reason and you didn't commit to traveling with them, or you can't travel at that point, let them know that you expect to be paid certain guaranteed hours per week. For example, most of the families I worked for used to go away around Christmas for two weeks, and I explained to them that my only resource of income was that job and that I couldn't go on unpaid for two entire weeks. Thankfully they all understood that and always paid me certain guaranteed hours. If you work 40 hours a week, ask for at least 30 hours guaranteed. There are families who travel two or more times a year. If you want, you can take your vacations while the family is traveling and be paid for them as your vacations. The problem arises when they travel during a time when there's no way you could take a vacation then for whatever reason. And last but not least, of course ask to be paid on the books. Hopefully, while you're talking to them they'll be writing down all this information.

Now in case you've gotten hired and the family talked to the agency first, talk to the agency and make sure they let the family know all the details of your work requirements. Some agencies, in order to place you, won't say all the details; some do, thankfully. However, on your first day of work, have a piece of paper with all the details so you can hand it to them to make sure they agree. It doesn't matter if it's not in a very official written form; you're trusting in their acknowledgment and that's good enough. I have to say that I've never had a written agreement like a contract with any of the families I worked for; it was all about our word and it worked well for me.

It's a personal decision. There are nannies who would choose to have a contract to feel protected. My protection was that I always knew that what I brought to every family I worked for was a great gift, and they were willing to do anything in order to keep that. I know from experience that some parents would feel uneasy signing written agreements, mostly high profile families. They feel that they only have to deal with the nanny agencies.

If you've been wondering all this time who in the world would hire you with all of these specific details, let me tell you that there are a lot of families willing to do it for the *right* person. And who is this *right* person? You!

After you've gone over all those details, it's your turn to narrate all the things you are committing to: staying with the family for at least three years, punctuality, responsibility, timely advance notice of doctor's appointments, vacations, or any other issue that may arise. Specify that you'll put the child on a schedule based on her daily routines and that you'll keep a written record of everything the child does through the day. Also commit to keeping the child's room tidy, helping with the child's laundry (time permitting), and cooking homemade food as first foods for the child as she grows, which is very easy. In the "Resources" section, I include a list of books for first foods ideas, vegan diets, vegetarian diets, etc.

Make sure to also say that you'd like to meet with parents throughout the year to discuss the child's issues and progress. Congratulations, you've got yourself a job!

CHAPTER 6

Work Environment— Relating to Co-workers

It's important to keep respectful and cordial relationships with all the people who work for the family. If you're hired by a single family, you'll most likely be around an assistant, housekeeper, and gardener. My advice to you is always be respectful, polite and courteous to all of them. Remember, they were there before you and they may be long-standing servers for the family.

If you're hired by a high-profile family, you'll definitely be working around more people; one or more chefs, two to three housekeepers, assistants, house managers and other nannies if there's more than one child in the family. Here things are a little bit more complex. It's like working at an office with lots of staff, and the thing is, all of them might have already engaged or want to engage with the children.

As I said in the introduction, I've worked in the LA area covering single families from Atwater Village, the San Fernando Valley, Hollywood Hills to the Westside, and Santa Monica to Pacific Palisades. Most of them were single families with both parents working out of the house or families that work from home. As the newly hired person for the child I met lots of housekeepers, gardeners, assistants, and always kept respectful interactions with all of them.

The housekeepers are excited about a new baby at home and want to play with him. They may even sometimes feel jealous of you. If you're caring for a toddler, they might even have a game going on with the child, maybe allowing him to step on the vacuum to get a ride while cleaning, etc. Because you're being respectful of them, you now can ask for the same respect in return by telling them to please not interact with the child if he's having a meal or a snack or if he's working on a game; the same applies to the assistants or gardeners. The parents will appreciate the harmony flowing through their house; no one likes to have a conflicting person giving all the wrong energy.

When working for high-profile families, many challenging situations will arrive. Personally out of all the jobs I had, these kinds were the most difficult to work at not because of the family or the child, but because of all the staff involved. Like the previous example of the housekeeper who is excited about the child and wants to engage with him, there are more people trying to do the same thing. For instance, you might be arriving home from the park and have a plan with the child to take his shoes off, change and go to the restroom, wash his hands, and then go to the dining table for lunch; but along the way, you encounter the assistant who starts talking to the child, then get to the kitchen and the chef starts offering lunch or showing the food to the child. At this point, the plan gets forgotten. The child of course gets distracted and now it's a struggle to get him to wash his hands.

If you wonder what's wrong with the staff trying to give some love to the child, I say nothing. That's not the point here. Of course everyone loves to see a child and engage a little, but for the sake of consistency and routine, we, with all due respect, kindly ask the staff not to engage the child as soon as they see him; to please wait and see what's going on first or at least ask you if it's a good time to engage the child. All this will make much more sense once you learn about the Educaring® Approach. You'll learn that it really takes so little to distract a child and put an end to some developmental thing going on at the moment. This is also true for the parents.

Another situation I also would like to discuss here is how to engage the child's loving grandparents. This can be very delicate to deal with. Grandparents are a part of the family who will come to visit or the child will visit. Sometimes the child is so used to you that when the grandparents visit, the child doesn't want to be or play with his grandparents. In this case, it's better to explain to the child that you will leave the room and be somewhere else so the grandparents can enjoy the child.

Other times when the grandparents come to visit, the child will get so excited that he won't want to stay with you, but with them. Here again it's better to back off and go chill out for a little and let them enjoy themselves. You'll find this usually happens when the grandparents are great spoilers and let the child do anything he wants, even the unthinkable. All the limits and rules will be broken and that's ok. You know why? Because they're the grandparents and can do as much as they want if the parents don't mind. I'd recommend for your sake leaving them alone in case something happens; you don't want to be held responsible. This might sound bad or extreme, but believe me. I've seen grandparents letting the kids ride bikes in the living room, have breakfast in bed, feed them while taking a bath, watch lots of TV, etc.

Still, you are very respectful, kind, and cordial with them at all times.

CHAPTER 7

WORK ETHICS

Yes, we're talking about work ethics here. I've seen such a lack of ethics in this matter when working as a nanny. I've seen nannies and families frustrated only because the schedule was changed without proper notice on both sides, coming to work late or leaving way past your time to go home, unpaid overtime, etc.

The fundamental word I like to use here is "respect." Respect means showing consideration for, treating courteously or kindly, paying proper attention to, not violating.

I'd also like to develop some ideas such as:

- Identifying with the family
- Having the heart of a servant
- Being a conflict solver
- Being non-judgmental
- Having faithfulness
- Having gratitude

The application of these concepts will allow you to be successful when working for any family.

As you've been reading, you've seen the word "respect" in many cases by now, but how do I apply this to work ethics? After you've been hired, there's something fundamental you need to start doing from day one: being punctual. Punctuality is key. At my last three-year job, which I recently finished, I might have been late five times, meaning five or ten minutes late, due to external situations such as traffic. Out of my 15 sick days throughout those three years, I used three. I don't say this to brag, but to show how I demonstrated respect. Respect is being punctual every day to work, never late, never a late notice that you won't come to work, not missing a day just because, not even getting sick because you take responsibility for your health. When you agree to a last-minute request, it's a solid yes. You won't change your mind in the next few hours; if you say no, it's no.

Respect is being polite and respectful with every single person at the house starting with the child, as we discussed. By giving respect you're not only teaching by example, but this is also your way of saying, "I expect the same from you." If you think about it, you're asking for something that you're giving first. So when the time comes for you to go home, you leave right on time, not 10 or 15 minutes late. You expect not to be told too late about any change to the schedule. You expect to be treated in the same way you treat others.

I've had nanny colleagues who would easily be late every day, work only four out of their five working days, and constantly miss a day. This behavior not only says so much about your work ethics, but it also creates confusion, inconsistency, and stress for the families and children you care for.

Identification with the family means you're willing and ready to stay for a long-term commitment, which is at least three years, for the child's sake. It's hard for the babies and families to be changing nannies. So in your head, you know this will be your job for at least the next three years. It also means that you'll do your best to accomplish your goal with the family: a healthy and well-understood child and a relationship with the family that has eternal value. You see yourself as part of the family. We the nannies go to the hearts of the families and live with them. Basically, we see their struggles, their happiness, their circumstances and more.

On the other hand, we do also have lives, but a life they don't see. Personally, I've never befriended any of my bosses. I've always maintained a professional relationship with them. I wouldn't tell them I just broke up with a boyfriend or something like that. Even when they were kind enough to ask about my daughter, I'd always reply, "She's good, thank you." I won't get personal and in my experience, this helped the relationship because parents will understand that they have a well-grounded individual helping their child. How would you like to have a nanny who seems to have so many issues in her personal life? How could she be of good help? Not only that, but the impact on the child is also great because children are like sponges; they can sense your feelings or emotions and can easily get affected in the wrong way. If you're going through any circumstance and need a couple of days, say so. Rest and get yourself together for your own sake and the sake of the child, and then go back to work.

Having the heart of a servant means exactly that. You're passionate about serving others. This has a lot to do with leadership; true leaders serve. You're always thinking, "What can I do to help them better?" Even though in Chapter 5, when discussing the contract I advised to be specific that you're a nanny and not a housekeeper-nanny, I have to say that while in the house and the child is sleeping, I would pick up a glass in the living room and take it to the dishwasher. I would pick up a piece of paper on the floor. I would take out the trash if it's in front of me and really overflowing, but without commitment—meaning "I was passing by and I saw it, so I did it." Like many would advise, go the extra mile. Believe me, in time it'll pay off. The idea is you're ready to help.

Being a conflict solver means that you don't always have to win; that in order to keep a peaceful environment, you're willing to concede or just not complain or say nothing about anything. Example: once, I was sent an email saying that every time I use the main gate, I shouldn't forget to lock it, the email sounded very commanding and not too polite. To worsen matters, I never used that gate but the back door because of the strollers, etc. I responded super kindly, "Thank you for letting me know, I will do as you say." I didn't run to my boss to complain or ever say anything about it to anyone. Another example, when you're asked last-minute about something, don't answer just yet. Say something like, "I'll check my schedule" or offer possible solutions if you have to say no. Even when you think you could do it wait because, speaking from experience, you may say yes and then not remember you have a doctor's appointment or some other commitment on the same date. Don't feel obligated to say yes all the time. Avoid conflict.

Non-judgment, means exactly that: to not judge. Working as a nanny means that you'll enter the heart of the family and will come to know everything about them, from what they do for a living, their personalities, their relatives and friends, and so on. As humans, the easy thing to do is start judging our employers' "dos" and "don'ts" and start wondering, "Why this? Why that?" I've done it. If there is *the* thing I could advise you to know about working as a nanny, it's be grateful of your job. Guard your words when referring to your employers and don't try to *fix* their lifestyle. We're not fixers, we're helpers.

Now why would I say that? Because no matter where I was, park, playground, class, or school, I'd always find a nanny who's unhappy about *one* thing (or more) about the job and always complained about something regarding her employers; about how they spoiled the children, were too nervous about the children falling, too picky about something, they won't ever be with the children, or about the children always crying when mommy is around. For whatever reason, at some point, there will always be a nanny complaining about the job.

This is what I believe. I'm a helper. I go to work, do my best, behave professionally, and go back home. Whatever thing I see, notice, or learn from my employers I respect. I try to understand and I know that I'm not there to judge or criticize them. I'm not God. I feel fulfilled by using the best of my knowledge around the child and knowing that the child's needs have been met and that as long I'm there, I'll be respected for what I do. I learned through the years that we're all different. We all come from different backgrounds, have different ways, manners, customs; we're different.

In my experience and because of my training in the Educaring® Approach, I learned how to be patient, observant, and calm as well as how to let the children be without interfering or interrupting them. I learned how not to engage children while they're playing. I learned how to allow children to entertain themselves. But I learned all of this with time and practice. So every time I'd get to a new home and when applying the principles, I'd find parents who in the beginning wouldn't understand or weren't able to engage that way.

Some of them were so amazed by the result in the child when treated that way that they were happy to learn and attend classes where they could be surrounded with other families practicing the principles of the Educaring® Approach. Others would just appreciate the wonders of a self-confident child, but wouldn't embrace it wholly and that was totally ok. We don't live in a perfect world. That's why I say my intention won't ever be to fix, somehow change, or push parents to do or follow exactly what I'm doing. What matters is that the child is engaged with respect and therefore, you impact her life forever.

Experience has shown me that after two years or more of applying the Educaring® Approach consistently, those children are in a position of understanding words and explanations of why things happen around them. They're secure, confident, engaging, with a sense of self, and their attention span was greater than that of most four-year-olds, despite being two years old.

In the past years, I was never concerned about leaving the children after these two or three years of service because I knew my job was done. Those children were ready to attend pre-school, and I knew I emptied myself into those children. I felt accomplished because I gave it all. And I also understood early on that I'm not the parent, that the child will be fine. Once, I was talking to a family about me leaving after fulfilling my three years and I said something like, "It's always my goal to finish well and make a difference in a child's life," and they said to me, "You did." This was actually a family that loved the Educaring® Approach but wouldn't embrace it fully due to their lifestyle. However, they did greatly appreciate seeing their son so self-confident, independent, and bright.

After the application of the Educaring® Approach principles during these three years of service, the child will become: "Secure, competent, confident, curious, cheerful, attentive, exploring, cooperative, peaceful, focused, self-initiating, resourceful, involved, inner-directed, and aware" (Gerber, Greenwald, Weaver 2013).

Having faithfulness: no matter what you do or where you work, there will be times when you want to run away from your job. Who doesn't at some point? The big difference dwells in staying, being committed. You're not a quitter, except of course if you're being mistreated or disrespected. In my experience, what makes nannies think about running away from their jobs is mainly the long hours or a demanding boss, but these scenarios mostly happen to nannies who didn't set their limits, or set the schedules and keep them. That's why in the beginning of the book we talked all about it, what you could and couldn't commit. Be a person who keeps his/her word, even when things don't go as planned. Be professional and fulfill your commitment.

Having gratitude: my godfather used to say gratitude is a heavy stone to carry around. Personally, I'm a spiritual being and every day I wake up grateful to be alive, to be healthy, grateful because I have a wonderful daughter, and grateful because I have a wonderful job. Having this energy every morning helps out through the day and everything just flows from that point on.

When we discuss the Educaring® Approach, you will see that we teach by modeling. For instance, I'd say thank you to the child every time the she does or accomplishes a small task, like allowing me to change her diapers, and so on. This will encourage the child to say "thank you" later on.

But going back to work ethics, be grateful. Recall that thanks to this family, you can eat and go on with your life. Don't even take little things for granted. For instance, if the mom happens to get home early and dismisses you, don't think, "Well, that's what she's supposed to do." No, she could well let you stay until the last minute, but if she lets you go early, say thank you and that you appreciate that. Or if you need to leave because something came up in your personal life and it's very understandable, don't have the attitude that your employers are supposed to let you go. Always say thank you for their understanding and that you appreciate it.

All of these things may sound so simple, but they make a big difference in your relationship with your employers.

CHAPTER 8

BUILDING UP YOUR RELATIONSHIP WITH THE PARENTS

This relationship began the day of the interview when you all got to meet each other. Respect is the foundation you want to lay down when building up the relationship with the parents. We have already discussed that you ask for respect by giving it first in every way, shape, and form. Being punctual every day means you expect to go home on time. Be respectful by always being professional and not trying to befriend your boss by telling him/her your personal issues no matter the subject. Be respectful by setting limits on your work hours and schedules. Be respectful by asking for days off with enough notice. Be respectful by always being calm, polite, and kind to all personnel involved in the household.

The other area of our relationship with the parents is in regards to the child. Something great I learned early as a nanny is to keep a book where I would write down everything the child did throughout the day; what time he ate, slept, pooped, went for a walk, went to the park, and so on. Parents like that very much because when they're back home and you're gone, they can check the notebook if they have questions about when the last time the child ate and so on.

In the same respect, whenever you get to work, after greeting the whole family, it's important for you to ask for a report of the night: how the child did through the night, if he had breakfast etc., so you can prepare for the day based on that. This may sound simple, but it's not; I've found moms who wouldn't be so willing to give the report for many reasons. Maybe because they're too tired early in the morning to talk about the bad night they just had or they simply don't feel like it. Others would tell you all about it. You somehow need to find out how the child's night went or how the day's been so far if you're the afternoon nanny in a household with several nannies. If we have a tired child due to a bad night, he probably won't be up for going to the playground, or may not be willing to cooperate or engage due to his tiredness. That's why it's important to keep a record of everything regarding the child.

Another thing I used to do when hired by a family is run a Google search for their names not because I'm nosey, but because I like to get to know what their jobs are so I can better understand the mechanics of the household. When I was working for a family of writers, one day I casually mentioned, "Oh, I've googled you," and the mom laughed, saying, "That's Larissa." She maybe thought, "She cares enough to find out," but to me it's more a way of trying to understand their lifestyles so I can go along with it.

For example, if one of the parents travels every week/month for a week or two, you learn to understand that the staying parent may feel tired, a bit overwhelmed, and may not be in a great mood every day. Also, when the absent parent returns, you prepare the child by letting him know that and when the family reunites again, you withdraw yourself a little bit. The child might want to only be with you because he's used to seeing you, but you have to give the child room, space to be. And you must use your best judgment.

Another great thing to help foster a relationship with the parents is having meetings with both parents to discuss their feelings about you as a nanny, anything else they'd like you to do or change, let them know how you're doing, and share any ideas you may have. Meetings are good to keep everyone on the same page. You can have them maybe every three months or twice a year. If you're able to see the parents and have a little chat every day, twice a year works great, but if you hardly see both parents, meetings should be scheduled more frequently, sometimes every eight weeks. Overall, try to keep the parents informed about the child's activities, what new milestones he has achieved and the new words, or new likes he enjoys such as food, games, etc.

If the parents, at some point get personal in sharing details about their lives with you, just listen. Don't try to give advice. Being a parent is overwhelming; sometimes they just need someone to listen. If it's something about the child, you'll always have something to say. For example, it's not uncommon that the children behave better with their nannies than with their parents. It's normal, at the end of the day when the parents are back home that the child will be a little fussy. It's his way of saying, "I missed you, Mom/Dad," perhaps.

Once while we were on a long trip, the mom was a little tired and overwhelmed. The children weren't cooperating much and all of a sudden, I heard her saying to the children, "Larissa does everything better than mommy." She sounded frustrated. I ran to where they were and said, "Never! No one is better than mommy." When this kind of situation happens, be sure to respond in a gentle way, but firmly establish who you are and who the parents are. Always be observant and use your best judgment.

If at some point you notice something different, speak up about it. One other occasion when working for another family, I heard the mom saying, "X was so happy with me until you got here." I didn't pay much attention in the beginning, but after hearing it three times, I asked to have a meeting and asked this mom upfront what she meant, and if there was something wrong. Don't be afraid. Speak up. Very respectfully state your opinions and reach to an agreement.

CHAPTER 9

BUILDING UP YOUR RELATIONSHIP WITH THE CHILD

Dr. Emmi Pikler once said, "The relationship is all. It is a matter of life to the baby" (The Pikler Collection 2011).

This relationship began the moment you met each other. Remember when you introduced yourself to the child as if you introduced yourself to another adult? From that point on, the family and the child knew it was going to be a completely different relationship, like no other.

The first thing to do as soon as you start working is to look for a safe environment for the child and you to be. Hopefully the house will be child-proofed. If not, you need to set up a safe environment. You'll learn more reasons why in the next chapter about the Educaring® Approach. Not having a place destined for the child to play brings all kind of issues. For example, you and the parents end up holding the child in your arms and carrying her everywhere, which isn't good for the child and for your back. Even worse, this invites parents to buy all kinds of bad toys such as bouncy chairs, walkers, and swings where the child is placed so the parents or the nanny can do their work or cook, etc. All these things don't help the child's natural development; on the contrary, they hinder development.

Another important thing to start doing is creating a routine from day one for the child and yourself. Day after

45

day, doing the same thing gives security to the child. She'll know what to expect, feel confident, and trust you. If your workday begins at 9 am, it's likely that the child has already eaten breakfast. So if she had a good night's sleep, she'll be ready to go for a walk, to the park, or simply ready to go to her playing area. Then, maybe it will be time for a bottle and a nap. After the nap, she'll be ready to eat again, maybe another bottle or lunch, After that, more playing time and then maybe a little snack until mom or dad comes back and it's time for you to go. What's important is doing the same thing over and over. The routine should only be changed when the child is ready, meaning that due to her natural development, the child no longer wants to take two naps a day. She'll move on to one nap after or before lunch. Same thing with food. She may move up to solid foods, be ready to attend a class, etc. It's very important for you to establish this connection with the child where the child gets to know you from doing the same things over and over again on a daily basis and having a routine.

In time, you'll discover that your relationship with the child will be very different from the relationship she has with her parents. For instance, the child will be rambunctious and not cooperative when mommy or daddy change her diaper, while with you, the child will lie down, be calm, and let you do it. I've seen parents so afraid of the diaper changing moment because it will be too stressful and drain all of their energy that they leave the poop in the diaper until I get to work every morning to do it. If you're a parent and recognize this scenario, I have to tell you that no matter how the diaper change turns out or if there's a lot of crying during it, you're the child's mom or dad and it's still necessary for you to do it. You'll soon learn that caregiving activities, diapering, feeding, and bathing are times of refueling and one-on-one time to reconnect, so I encourage you to by all means do it! For tips on changing diapers, I highly recommend my friend and mentor, Janet Lansbury's, blog (See "Resources").

Monday mornings, children are usually tired because they were out and about with their parents over the weekend and you may find new things she's been given or new things she's been allowed to do. One time, I came back to work on a Monday morning to find the baby I cared for playing with golf clubs that were twice his size, heavier than he could handle and dangerous to drag around. The only thing I said was, "I see you're holding a golf club. I'd like to hold onto them," waited, and then removed it from the baby's hands and asked him what would he like to play with instead. After that, I managed to put the golf clubs away and did not allow the baby to play with them anymore. My message is, "You can play with golf clubs with mommy and daddy, but not with Larissa." On other occasions, I've found the child jumping on the bed or climbing high places. I still won't allow the child do it while in my care all for her safety. You can totally discuss issues like this with parents and explain your reasoning.

Throughout this relationship, you'll realize that the child eats better with you, falls asleep faster with you, changes diapers easier with you, not to say that you're better than the parents. Not at all. It's all due to applying the Educaring® Approach, which you'll soon learn all about. And caretakers do have an unbiased point of view. We can have an objective opinion and don't feel the pressure parents have because these are their children.

However, in families who work as a team applying the same principles, things will flow very differently, but diaper changing still isn't perfect. Every day is different and it changes as the child grows up and starts walking. You'll learn more about all this in the next chapter about the Educaring® Approach.

What I'd like to point out here is that while being a nanny, you'll spend long hours with this child five days a week, leaving the parents with weekends and nights maybe after 5 pm so they have roughly three hours to bathe and put the child to sleep. So you'll be the one who's with the child most of the time. Think about it for a moment, about the impact of your presence in the child's life. Enjoy the children you take care of today. You'll be forever in their memories and they'll stay forever in your heart.

PART TWO

CHAPTER 10

THE EDUCARING® APPROACH

It's time to discuss Magda Gerber's Educaring® Approach and the organization she co-founded, Resources for Infant Educarers® (RIE®) (pronounced "wry"). Before we start learning about RIE®, I'd like to introduce to you to the creator and founder of RIE®: Magda Gerber. A lot has been said about Magda and her work, and more and more people are starting to know and share her work and practice it. This book intends to introduce Magda's work in an understandable and easy way that will help you realize the importance of applying the Educaring® Approach principles when raising a child. We'll develop each one of them and that will leave you with some understanding and if you desire to further pursue your learning, you'll also know where to start.

I'm grateful for her love, dedication, and hard work in standing strong about her different point of view of children. I'm also grateful I was able to get to know her work 11 years ago, understand it, apply it, and make it my own. The principles of the Educaring® Approach will make a huge difference in your work as a nanny, as you'll find it rewarding, stress-free, and will produce well-understood children and contented parents. Not only that, but you'll transcend from a well-intended caregiver to an Educarer. You'll know how.

Here's a glimpse of Magda's life and work:

Magda Gerber, world-renowned child therapist and infant specialist, developed a revolutionary philosophy of infant care based on treating infants with respect and trust in their abilities to develop naturally at their own pace.

Born in Hungary and educated at the Sorbonne in Paris, Magda came to the United States with her husband and three children in 1957, after fleeing her native Budapest in the aftermath of the Hungarian Revolution.

She became fascinated with infant care, first as a young mother, and later through the teachings of her children's pediatrician, friend and mentor, Dr. Emmi Pikler.

After years of observing and interacting with infants, Magda gained a unique understanding of how parents, caregivers and professionals can nurture the development of genuine, authentic babies by encouraging their spontaneity and drive to learn and discover on their own. Many of her ideas were simple common sense such as the importance of giving full attention and engaging the infant during everyday care giving activities like feeding, bathing and diapering. Yet these ideas were unconventional when she began to introduce them in the United States in the early 1970's. Today, Magda's methods have become accepted and commonly practiced by professionals, caregivers and parents, and have influenced the guidelines set forth by the National

Association for Young Children (NAEYC), the credentialing agency that promotes high standards for quality group care for infants and toddlers.

In 1973, Magda Gerber co-founded with pediatrician and clinical professor Thomas Forrest, M.D., the non-profit organization Resources for Infant Educarers (RIE) in Los Angeles, California. RIE was one of the first places in the U.S. offering a specialized environment for infant observation and parent education ("In Memoriam" 2012).

Through Magda Gerber we learn that the best way to teach values like honesty, generosity, empathy and forgiveness is to model, rather than force . . . One of the greatest gifts Magda bestows on us is the knowledge that infants are self-learners. And this is how a parent or caregiver spells *relief*. Self-learning means we don't need to provide any lessons for a baby, and we need not feel pressured by developmental timetables. Infants are internally motivated to learn the things they need to learn: motor skills, communication, problem solving. We provide the foundation of a secure relationship with a caring adult, a safe environment conducive to exploration and discovery, and let nature take its course. We never have to worry that we are not doing 'enough,' or that the child isn't doing 'enough.' Whatever a healthy infant or toddler chooses to do in his safe environment is the perfect curriculum for him on any particular day. We let go of 'doing', and are left with observing, learning, enjoying . . .

Thanks to Magda Gerber our daily experience with children is profoundly enriched. She challenges us to hone our observational skills like scientists, listen to another's feelings without judgment like psychotherapists, and empty our minds to revel in the moment like Zen Masters.

She teaches us to make creative decisions about when and how to intervene so as not to interrupt a child's process of discovery, and work to be models of authenticity by staying connected to our true selves and Magda's most splendid gift of all is a simple truth: child care is the developing relationship of understanding between two distinct human beings (Lansbury 2010).

Magda Gerber died in her home surrounded by her children on April 27, 2007. ("In Memoriam" 2012)

When I learned about Magda Gerber's work they used to call her work RIE®. Now they call it the Educaring® Approach. The first time I learned about the Educaring® Approach was back in 2001. The family I worked for was following the Educaring® Approach. I didn't know anything about it when one day, my boss said, "Let's go to RIE® class," and off we went. When we got there, I saw this big empty space like a yoga studio surrounded by mirrors and I noticed everyone arriving spoke in a very quiet soft voice, greeting each other and the babies. The instructor was, Wendy Kronick, who soon became my first RIE® teacher and to this day I hold dearly as a friend. Wendy was setting up the room by laying a white sheet on the floor and placing objects like soft cloths and small wooden objects on top. She was quiet too. Each parent started to sit down quietly around the mat covered with the sheet forming a circle and just placing the babies on their backs. No one talked, and the instructor just narrated whatever the babies did.

Everyone seemed to be just observing their babies. At some point, Wendy told us when observation time was over and asked us what we observed. Parents started saying things like, "I saw Jason enjoying his thumb for the first time," "Kenya began rolling last week and now it's all she wants to do," "When Jason touched Kenya with his foot, Kenya stopped and looked," and so on. I thought, "This is crazy! Paying money to come to a class where you do *nothing* is a waste of money!" Later on as I read the books, everything made sense little by little and I also started developing the *muscle* of observation.

The Educaring® Approach is an approach based on *respect*. One day, I understood that because I respect the child, I don't handle him as an object; I speak to the child about everything I do unto him and when he's playing, I won't sweep him off the floor without telling him. I won't teach him how to play or what to do with the object he's playing with. Because I respect him, I find joy in letting him solve his little challenges like finding a ball that rolled away. I won't rush to help him as if he was a handicapped person. I see the child as a resourceful human being even when he's so small.

Because I respect him, I will set up an environment where he can be safe and free to explore every corner without getting hurt. Because I respect him, I'm consistent in every daily routine so he can feel secure and trust that this is what happens every day in his life until the changes come naturally, not forced by me. This includes not putting the child into positions that he's not ready for, such as sitting, standing, or crawling. Because I respect him, I won't try to shut him down when he's crying, but acknowledge his crying and tell him it's ok to cry if he needs to cry. I'll be patient listening to him until he feels relief and stops by himself.

I never really thought about the true meaning of respect until I found the Educaring® Approach. Think about all the things we do to children from not knowing better. We pass them as objects from hand to hand. We try to help them at all times thinking they can't do anything by themselves because they're children. We try to stop them from crying because we tend to think something's wrong and we can't stand crying. We teach them what to do with their toys because we're bigger and know better. We rush through every caring activity like diapering, feeding, and bathing because the child fusses and we better get it done or else he'll cry harder. We are scared of a crying child. We never see or respect the child's point of view.

And that's when we end up tired, frustrated, and disappointed because after we have tried to do all things possible to have a "happy child," entertaining and indulging every little peep from the child, kaboom! We become slaves, because there's no way a child can be happy 24 hours a day, seven days a week and you can't either!

One of the breakthrough moments in my life happened during my Educaring® Approach training. The instructor was explaining respect and asked us to think about two moments in our lives when we were or felt really respected, and another moment in our life when we felt disrespected. The most important thing was discussing the feelings these two situations brought to us. Everyone in the class talked about it, but what struck me most was discussing the feelings it brought when we felt disrespected: ignored, abused, let alone, misunderstood, rejected, abandoned, not loved, disregarded, sad, depressed, furious, mad, angry. Everyone had something negative to say about feeling disrespected. However, the feelings when respected were: acknowledged, happy, understood, peaceful, a sense of worth, loved, that someone cared, important, confident, resourceful, competent, secure, aware, and cheerful.

Now think about it for a moment. We aren't different from children. We as adults can identify those feelings and talk about them. Children aren't always able to talk about them, but that doesn't mean they don't feel it or sense little things, like the hands of a caretaker rushing to finish the task, the absent face of a mother talking on the phone while nursing her baby, the constant overstimulation with toys or entertaining devices, swings, etc.

Throughout the pages of this book you've heard me talk about respect, and how to establish a respectful relationship with co-workers, employers, family members, and the child. Basically by doing or following the simple advice, you were learning how to apply the Educaring® Approach, which brings us to our next chapter.

CHAPTER 11

How to Apply the Educaring Approach

Before we commence talking about the "how," think about this statement: "The seed of natural development is in every living being; be it plant, animal or human it does not need to be 'helped' to develop" (Selver 1994).

The application of the Educaring® Approach principles are based on that statement. I don't want to talk about child development here, but it's very well known that there are charts to follow the development of children from birth, and if by any chance a child is a little bit behind, the parents grow concerned. Let me tell you here that every child is unique and has her own developmental pace of growth. Magda Gerber used to say: "Trust that your baby will develop in her own time, rhythm and manner. After all, who knows better how to be a baby than a baby?" (Gerber 2013)

Let's take a closer look at the Educaring® Approach principles. The Educaring® Approach is a philosophy to raise children based on:

- Basic trust in the child to be an initiator and self-explorer
- An environment for the child that is physically safe, cognitively challenging, and emotionally nurturing
- Time for uninterrupted play
- Freedom to explore and interact with other infants

- Involvement of the child in all caregiving activities to allow the child to become an active participant rather than a passive recipient
- Sensitive observation of the child in order to understand his or her needs (Present, aware, interested, and available)
- Consistency and clearly defined limits and expectations to develop discipline(Gerber, Owen, Petrie 2005)

Now let's see how we put these principles into practice:

"Basic Trust in the Child to Be an Initiator and Self-Explorer"

The way you see the child is very significant here. The person who believes a child is competent will interact and care for that child in a very different way than the person who believes that the child is helpless. How do you let the child be an initiator and self-explorer? By letting her take the lead about what she wants to do. For example, when you get to work every day, do not have a "plan" of what to teach or what to do to entertain the child, but instead get there with a sense of wonder. You can say, "I wonder what you'd like to do or play with today," and wait.

Whenever it's your start time at work, keep in mind that the child has been with the parents, and usually, if the child is an infant, the parents will hold her all the time. If the child's not an infant she will probably be entertained a lot, until you, by modeling, can teach the parents that they need to trust that the child can be an initiator. Try to establish a transitioning time, the time when you start taking over for the parents. If the child fusses about going to your arms and leaving mom's, explain to her what's going on. You can say,

"Are you ready to come to me?" and wait, then say, "It's hard to let go of mommy sometimes. Now we'll both go to our playing area to start our day." If you do this consistently, the child will know every morning that that's what happens.

Then take the child to the hopefully safe environment she has in the house. When going to the playing area, walk slowly so the child can take in what's going on. Once you're in the playing area still holding her, sit down and sit the child on your lap, and when she's ready, she'll want to let go of your arms and start playing. You can help the child by always laying her on her back, even if she's able to sit up by herself. Let the child know that your time together has begun and that you'll take her to play. Explain that you'll lay her down on her back, wait, and then do it. Place the child on the floor and let her be, you can just sit on the floor next to her to show the child your availability in case she needs you.

If the child is an infant and not moving much, you can place some objects close to her to see if she's interested in playing with them and observe. If the child crawls, you can just let her be. The child will go wherever she wants to reach the toys she wants to play with.

And if the child is a toddler, the same. Take her to the playing area and let the child choose what to play with, or maybe invite her outside to the yard. Going outdoors applies from infants to toddlers. Children need to spend time outdoors from the very beginning. As infants, they can be taken outside to change the environment and get some fresh air, always placed on a blanket and on their backs. Going outdoors also switches moods and invigorates children.

A Safe, Challenging, Predictable Environment

Families don't have to child-proof the whole house, at least not until the baby starts moving A safe environment for the child to be in can be created even in a small home. You can create a place that can be fenced close to the dining room or in the living room.

From zero to two months, children spend time in their cribs or playpens. When the child becomes more mobile, we need to create a safe environment. As I said, we can gate a small area in the house and place the child's favorite toys or objects for her to play with. This area must be physically safe, meaning there won't be even one object that could hurt the child.

A challenging environment is a place where, as the child grows and becomes more mobile, her development can constantly continue. You may offer a wooden structure for her to claim if she's ready and wants to; we have to be sensitive about what kind of toys we offer by providing toys or objects suitable for the child's age, soft objects that the child can have a good grip of but aren't small enough to fall through a toilet paper roll (choking hazard).

You'll realize children get frustrated and start fussing around an object they can't manage properly. Once, a baby I cared for was trying to hold a Russian doll (the ones that open and have smaller dolls inside). He was drawn to the doll and tried really hard to hold it, but it was too big and slippery. He became frustrated, so I got closer to him, explained that the object was still a little big for his hands and that I was going to put it away because it looked like he was getting upset. I waited and did it. We should avoid presenting objects that the child isn't ready for as much as possible so we won't find ourselves constantly saying, "No, you can't touch that." Think about it. How would you feel if you were given a huge object to play with? You'd probably try to play with it, but soon enough you'll get tired and frustrated.

Our goal as nannies should be to offer passive toys (ball, rag doll, rings, wooden objects, etc.) to the children as much as possible, to make active children. Active toys make passive children, TV being the biggest active toy! Passive toys are objects that the child can manipulate in many ways and that don't require much adult help or supervision, a toy that's easily cleaned and of different sizes, shapes, colors, weight, and material.

"Time for Uninterrupted Play"

Whenever the baby is not sleeping or involved in caregiving activities, like eating or diapering it is time for uninterrupted play. To be able to provide uninterrupted play the child must have a space that is completely safe, a safe environment to be. We will see this in the correspondent principle.

This principle is sometimes hard to put into practice, since as nannies, we've been given the idea that we have to entertain the child, play with her and make her smile and be happy. I had the chance to interpret a class for nannies at the Los Angeles RIE® Center twice and both times when we asked the nannies what was difficult to understand about the Educaring® Approach, they all said "not entertaining the child," or "not playing with the child," because they were afraid that their employers would think they didn't like or love the children they took care of. But the truth is, by teaching a child how to play or what to play with, we hinder their inner curiosity and self-motivation. Magda Gerber said, "Be careful what you teach. It might interfere with what they are learning." (RIE® Website 2013)

Uninterrupted time for playing means that once you've provided the safe environment and you've begun to see the child as resourceful, an initiator, and a self-explorer, you sit, relax, and watch the child do her wonders without interrupting, meaning you don't teach to play or play with her. Remember my first experience with an Educaring® class? That's exactly what you do: "nothing" but observe. I put the word "nothing" in quotes because the truth is, it's not "nothing." You're actually doing a lot in the sense that you're being present, physically and emotionally. By sitting near the child, you say, "I'm here for you if you need me and I'm here enjoying watching all the things you are able to do in this stage of your life," "I respect you so I won't interrupt you or help you unless you ask for it."

However depending on the child's age there will be moments during the uninterrupted play time that you will engage the baby and interact together sharing joyful moments. She may hand you a toy or a book she would like you to read to her, or offer you a cup, or talk to you, these interactions are very important to their emotional development.

When I first started doing this—laying the child on her back with small objects and soft cloths around and sitting close to watch what she did—it was a total eye-opening experience for me. I realized children and babies can do more than we think. Their inner ability to concentrate on one thing, like holding onto a little object for so long (up to twenty minutes sometimes!) just turning it around, banging it on the floor, putting it in their mouths, and shaking it. It really amazed me. Time flies and the next thing you know it's lunchtime or naptime. I didn't have to "entertain" the child or carry her in my arms around the house because she was "bored" and therefore, I didn't get exhausted. Not only that, but the child didn't lose the chance to have healthy growth and development. There's so much brain development going on while the child holds that object for so long! If the only thing we do is hold the child in our arms, we restrict her body from developing. When children are placed on their backs, they can lift their legs up, kick, move, and more, while in our arms they can't.

There are a few reasons why a child can be interrupted while playing. Safety is one reason. For example, when she tries to pull a book from a tall shelf and the book could fall on her head. Interruption is also needed for a diaper change. Maybe she pooped while playing. Another reason could be because time is up and lunch or snack is next.

If you need to interrupt, apologize to the child for interrupting because we respect her. In Educaring® classes, I learned that when a child is to be interrupted, we need to address the situation as if we were interrupting an adult reading the newspaper.

The last thing to know about uninterrupted play time is to avoid praise. For example, if the baby accomplished putting a cube through a hole, or put her book back to the shelf, avoid saying "good job", "clever girl", "big boy." Instead you can replace those with acknowledgments of achievements and activities by using: "you did it," "I saw that," "you are enjoying jumping," "you wrote your name, you must be very proud of yourself," "you shared, that was very kind of you."

Children at play don't need praise for their actions. If we have something to say to everything they do or accomplish we are adding judgment; let the child's inner joy be self-motivating.

"Freedom to Explore and Interact with Other Children"

This is part of what's described above. When you don't interrupt playing time, the child has freedom to explore, figure out, learn, try out, discover, and so on. The interaction with other infants would most likely happen if you attend infant classes, or with a sibling. It's also very important not to interrupt interactions unless either of the children could clearly be hurt or struggles. For instance, we need to intervene when an infant who doesn't crawl yet gets one of her arms stuck, we let the child try to figure it out for a while and then if she's getting upset, we pick her up.

During my Practicum at the RIE® Center, I learned a lot about selective intervention. I served as a Practicum student in a toddler class, children aged 20 to 24 months old. At some point while playing, two children would want to play with the same object so many times and I remember Janet, the instructor, just letting the children try to figure it out by themselves. I saw that the engaging children would look to make eye contact with their parents to see if their parents were noticing the situation. The parents would just maybe nod their heads and say, "I see." The instructor would come closer and say, "I see you both want the ball." The children, still holding the ball, would just look at each other, talk, in their own way and sooner or later one of them would let the ball go. When the child who let go walked away, the child who kept the ball would many times follow the child who walked away and voluntarily offer the ball back to him/her! Isn't that amazing? If we as nannies or parents in charge are constantly hovering, and fixing every single interaction among our children we basically rob them of their chance to grow, figure out, and to bring forth what they are!

"Involvement of the Child in All Caregiving Activities to Allow the Child to Become an Active Participant Rather Than a Passive Recipient"

Remember how I wrote in the beginning that during job interviews I would say, "I would treat the child with respect and that I would always let her know everything I'm going to do before I do it unto her"? This includes explaining caregiving activities. Caregiving activities are: feeding, diapering, bathing and sleeping.

This is how you apply this principle: Prepare the environment ahead of time. Before involving the baby, have everything ready so you won't have to search for anything, such as cream, or water, which would disrupt your continuity together. Observe what the infant is doing. If she is absorbed playing, do not interrupt her, but wait for the right moment to intervene, then explain to the infant what you'll do. Although the infant may not understand your words at first, she will soon begin to associate your sounds and tone of voice with your gesture and actions, and develop her anticipation for enjoyable time shared together with her caregiver. You can say something like, "I see you're playing with your toys but you pooped and I need to change your diaper." Then wait a few seconds and say something like, "I'm picking you up now," wait for a few seconds then pick the child up and take her to the changing table.

Communicate with the child. Gently, with an apology for interrupting, ask for any play object in the infant's hands, explaining what you are doing. Reach and wait for a response. Don't pick up a child unexpectedly or from behind.

Explain and show the infant what you're going to do, step by step. You can say, "I'm opening your diaper now. I see there is a poop. These are the wipes," Show the wipes to her, and say, "I'm ready to wipe you now," wait and then wipe the child. You can say it may feel a little cold, and then, thank the child for letting you wipe her. As you remove the diaper, you can say, as you show it to the baby, "This is your soiled diaper. I'm putting it in the trash can now." Keep narrating what happens, "This is your new clean diaper. I'm putting it on you now," and so on. Allow the infant to respond and become involved in the process by making eye contact, studying your face, vocalizing, initiating play, following your actions and responding to you and you to her. Take your time. Slow down.

If the child you're taking care of is a toddler and can stand and refuses to lay down for the change of diaper you can change her standing up.

"Sensitive Observation of the Child in Order to Understand His/Her Needs" (Present, Aware, Interested, and Available)

In order to achieve what I described above, sensitive observation is needed. There isn't really a definition for these two words together, but I've understood sensitive observation as being fully present in body and mind when with the child, but from an objective position, being as calm as possible, not judgmental, and ready to respond to the child's cues, signs, and needs.

Being present in body means that whenever you're ready or know that it's your time to be with the child, you've already used the bathroom, finished all your chores, etc. You've got all you need so you know you won't get up from there in a while, unless the child needs a diaper change or to be fed of course. Hopefully, you're allowed to have observation time with the child and don't have to do many chores around the house. This allows us to practice what we said in the interview; you're a nanny, not a housekeeper and your focus is the child.

Being present in mind means you come to the child with a sense of wonder and excitement to see what the child's up to, what new thing she will do, what new body movements will happen today. Your mind is filled with the word and understanding of respect and you're calm because you know what you're doing. Moreover, because you're an objective individual, you come to the child believing that whatever the child does by then is exactly what her body is ready to do, therefore, she does it. For example, if the child tries to roll onto her side and her little arm gets stuck under her body, you might be tempted to help, but you don't, as I said you let the child try to figure it out for a while and then if she's getting upset, you pick her up. Natural development happens naturally.

Keep calm with the child. You don't sit next to the child, squealing because you can't take it anymore; "it's so cute" and you feel like squeezing the child in your arms, picking her up, and kissing her all over! I understand there's a strong inclination to touch and feel the child (they can be really adorable!), but remember we don't go around hugging, kissing, or touching people because we think they're cute. So why would we do that to the child? Showing affection is ok, but there's a moment for everything. And I'm not talking about the parents—I'm talking about us, the nannies. Parents are allowed to show all the love they have for the child and siblings and grandparents anytime, but really coming to the child, allowing the child to just be for a moment is the greatest gift we can offer. This is what I call true love. Someone who loves you doesn't just kiss you all the time. This someone cares and respects you so much that he or she lets you be.

After coming to the child in this state of mind, your eyes will discover all the wonders about children and how much they are capable of doing. Your perception will change forever.

Observation takes time and practice, slow down, be available but don't interfere unnecessarily, watch and learn and appreciate the infant as she plays.

"Consistency and Clearly Defining Limits and Expectations to Develop Discipline"

Magda Gerber once said, "The easiest way to develop good habits in general is to have a predictable daily life" (Gerber 1984) This can be achieved with a routine and schedule for naps, meals, and play time. Knowing what to expect when the child sees your face every morning is such an accomplishment for you and will produce a confident child who trusts you.

Setting limits will come easily because there's a routine and expectations on both the child's and your side. It also has to do with our behavior. We model the behavior for the child to emulate. We teach gentleness by being gentle. We say "please" and "thank you" to the child so later on, she'll say it back to us because we modeled it first. When setting limits, you must speak in first person. This tells the child who you are and what your limits and rules are, which may be different from the parents'. Remember my story of finding the child playing with golf clubs one morning? Well, I said, "I don't want you playing with the golf clubs," even though the parents would let the child do that in my absence because they *are* the parents. You also don't need to give a lengthy explanation for why you're not letting the child play outside or why you're not letting her hit a sibling, etc. If you take care of a young child, you can say, "Gentle, gentle" and with an older child, you can say, "I don't want you to hit me," or "I don't want you to play with my glasses." Sometimes you have to set the limit over and over again until the child internalizes the limit and becomes self-disciplined.

It is my hope that you find these concepts to make sense. You can find resources for taking Educaring® courses to fully understand in later sections of this book. It'll make a big difference in your career as a nanny.

CHAPTER 12

WHERE TO LEARN THE EDUCARING APPROACH

I started this book telling you about how I became a nanny kind of by accident and how when this particular family introduced me to the Educaring® Approach, I started reading the books and attending Parent-Infant Guidance™ classes. I became more and more interested by the great impact that a caregiver can have in the life of a young child. All of this encouraged me to take the classes and training to enrich my knowledge and not just because of that great impact, but because it also changed my life.

You can learn more about this wonderful approach at the RIE® Center in Los Angeles, if you live in LA of course, and by visiting *www.rie.org*. They offer pre-natal classes, such as "Before Baby™," "Parent-Infant Guidance™," "RIE® Professional Development," "Nurturing Nanny™," and "Cuidadoras Cariñosas™," which I had the opportunity to interpret into Spanish a couple of times.

CHAPTER 13

MISHAPS OF THE EDUCARING° APPROACH

When I use the word "mishaps," I'm not referring to the Educaring® Approach itself, but about some myths about Educaring® practices that have caused a stir because people got it wrong. This article from *The Daily Beast* is a good example.

> Little-known outside academic circles, the RIE philosophy has spread among parents via word-of-mouth. It has its own tight-knit circle of instructors; its own rituals (the narration of the diaper change); its own spare aesthetic (no mirrors, no dangling mobiles, no *Baby Einstein*); and its own set of guidelines (no singing, no rocking, no playpens). All of this honors the baby's "struggle" and builds a more "authentic self," proponents believe. RIE toys are simple—a paisley scarf, a wooden spoon, a plastic colander—so as to stimulate imagination and motor skills. And baby days are calm; there's no running multiple errands with the little one in tow . . .
>
> Beyond books and manuals, though, advocates consider the method a way of life. People talk about "doing RIE," said Memel, "But it's just an attitude, an awareness, a mindfulness." There are some, however, who see RIE as a parenting cult

that makes extreme and ridiculously inconvenient demands of modern parents (Piccalo 2010).

Though the Educaring® Approach is not yet well-known, I hope this book will bring people to practice the Educaring® Approach. And yes, the Educaring® Approach spreads by word-of-mouth through parents who took Parent-Infant Guidance™ classes and believe it's worth passing along because it works with their children. Yes, it has a tight-knit circle of instructors because the Educaring® Approach makes sure that the instructors out there are qualified to teach and have gone through a deep internalization of the principles and why they apply these principles. Educaring® courses aren't offered as a career where you get your diploma and you get to teach, but as a long journey of learning. It's been 11 years since I've started learning the Educaring® Approach and I'm still learning.

Narrating the diaper change isn't anything else besides modeling respect for the baby. Remember from the interview that I said I would explain everything I do and explain it throughout? This is because the child isn't an object and shouldn't be handled like one. Have you ever gone to get a pap smear? Don't you feel better when the nurse or Ob-Gyn lets you know everything he/she does to you? Think about the opposite. How would you feel?

The spare aesthetic is just the "safe environment" that we talked about, a place free of any objects that could hurt the child, a safe place for the child to be. There are no dangling mobiles because we are not to decide or impose what the child should stare at. The main use for those mobiles is for the child to look at them so the parent or caregiver can go on doing something else. Instead of talking to the child and explaining what's going on. And no *Baby Einstein* because more and more, we realize how bad it is for children to be put in front of the TV or video devices.

The Educaring® Approach even encourages some of the things this article says it prohibits. Yes singing, yes rocking, as a shared, pleasurable experience when not used as a tool to distract the child from a true, honest feeling or any other circumstance surrounding the child, such as the parent leaving, etc. Yes, playpens. They're ideal to have close to wherever the mom or caregiver is while taking care of the child, until the child becomes more mobile and needs a bigger place to be.

We also discussed the kinds of toys by simply stating that passive toys make active children and active toys make passive children, just take a look at children in front of the TV—they don't even blink! So, to me more than a philosophy or a method, the Educaring® Approach has been a common sense lifestyle when taking care of child.

This closes Part Two. If you'd like to learn more about the Educaring® Approach, please refer to the "Resources" section of the book.

MISCELLANEOUS

CHAPTER 14

TRAVELING WITH THE FAMILY

Nannies are sometimes required to travel with the family. This will most likely happen when working for a high-profile family. In my case, I always introduced myself as a single parent with no or little chances to accommodate trips. However, I did travel. There were families who invited my daughter along and I was grateful for that, but very cautious when accepting. The times I said yes to these circumstances were because the family would go to a hotel where I would have a separate room away from the family, the child was almost two years old at the time, and the family was going to play golf so I knew it was going to be the child, my daughter, and I hanging out for a few days. Plus the parents would want to be with their child after 5 pm.

I could also accommodate staying at the family house for a weekend or so with my daughter while the parents had a little weekend getaway. There were also families who, because of the demands of their work, had both parents travel unexpectedly. I remember one family left their young baby at my house for a few days. I'm sure that was the hardest decision for the parents to make. Their relatives lived in another country and they had no one to leave the child with. I'm grateful now that they entrusted me with their treasure. Be ready and willing to serve and help this may happen to you. Here in LA, when you're working for a family who travels three to five times a year and for more than a few days or sometimes for months, you could be in London one month, spend six weeks in Australia, or one week in Tel Aviv and the next one in New York. Phew! That's a lot of traveling!

But if this is happening, it's no surprise to you because you previously discussed all issues regarding traveling, such as the pay rate when traveling, if you said yes to traveling. Is the pay rate going to be the same? Any overtime payment? Any per diem? How many hours are you willing to work? When working in the family's home, you have a schedule, but let me tell you that when traveling, there is *no* schedule. Children's naps and meals may be altered because of time changes, and parents may or may not be present.

Let's look at possible settings. A vacation trip: you'll most likely go to a hotel and you may be given a room inside the family's suite or another room close to the family's room. A work trip: you may be in a hotel or the family may rent a house if they're staying for a long period of time. If this is the case, it would be good for you to request staying at a hotel close to the house, if possible of course; after working long hours (maybe 8 am to 9 pm) you'll appreciate being able to leave the house for some fresh air, some coffee, or just some rest without feeling like you're in some sort of prison. Plus, the house would have to be huge for you not to hear the family after you've finished working. If a hotel room isn't possible, just explain that you need to go to rest at certain time during the day.

To any parents who might be reading this part and wondering about it, think about having a hard-working helper with you through the day. If he/she doesn't have proper rest, it'll be chaos for the children and the family because often on trips, you may not sleep well every night. So it gives peace of mind to know that early in the morning, a refreshed, energetic, happy nanny will walk through your door to help you up. The hotel room is for the nanny's sake when traveling. Now let's see what to do for the children's sake when traveling.

Children are at the mercy of the parents until they reach adulthood. I'm not saying this in a bad way; it's a fact. If a family consists of a parent who travels a lot, the family has two options: the traveling parent going away and not seeing the family for a while or taking the whole family wherever mommy or daddy has to be at the time, regardless of the child's age. They will be tagged along the way. The trip is not a big deal if the child is between zero and six months old. They most likely sleep on the airplane, although the cabin pressure may bother their ears. If the child is more than six months old, it gets a little bit harder, especially if it's a long flight.

The best we can do as nannies is to prepare the child by letting him know that the whole family will soon be on a trip. We can do so by reading books about traveling and airplanes, visiting grandpa or grandma, and looking at pictures of the places you'll visit. This should be done by everyone involved in the trip, but not to the point of stressing the child about it. Make sure to talk about it in a peaceful and happy voice. If you're required to pack the child's clothes, it's a very good idea to bring stuff that the child's used to or toys he's been playing with lately, maybe a blanket, a lovey, teddy, toy or an adored book.

For plane time, infants will most likely sleep and soothe with nursing, but for children six months and older, you may want to bring their favorite food (airplane food has no good options for children). If the child is on a specific diet, even more reason to bring the child's own food. It's also a good idea to bring some books to read, maybe a few toys, and a lot of patience and calmness because the child will cry at some point and you need to be ready to help the parents handle it. You might be the calm voice with a peaceful face acknowledging the child's feelings. Say, "I know it's a long flight and I see you're getting a little tired," or "We'll get there very soon." Maybe you could get up for a bit and walk her around. The most important thing is that you knew this was going to happen at some point and now you're ready to handle it.

Nowadays, parents use devices such as DVD players, laptops, etc. If this is the case, respect that. If you ask me, I wouldn't do it and I don't support watching TV or videos at all. It didn't happen while the children were under my care every day that I worked, but after I went home at 5 pm, it was the parent's choice and I respected that. What was important to me was to set the limits when the child was under my care. It's understandable that parents have a hard time listening to their children cry and therefore they offer them the choice of watching a video. Remember what I said about your ethics; we are not to judge, criticize or impose our rules over the family. Although I have to recognize that the use of these devices could be helpful for long flights.

When you finally arrive to the trip's destination, observe the child and think about what to do next. Maybe the child will be up to a warm bath to relax. Or maybe he'll be ready for sleep or some good food. Regardless of the choice, remember that even though the child might not show tiredness, he is indeed tired. Trips and flights are exhausting for grown-ups, so imagine how much more exhausting they are for children. They will need to rest for sure.

And then go with the flow. It's a trip where you're away from home and things will be different, the setting and hours etc., but you want to keep up the Educaring® Approach when engaging the child. Remember, always let him have uninterrupted time to play, narrate diaper changes, etc. If some other relatives are present around the child, let them be. For example, when the grandmother comes to visit, let them be. I'd walk away and go sit somewhere else and relax, but of course I'd keep my ears open in case they call or need me. When the children are young, they would often rather stay with you because they're used to you, but as they grow when grandma arrives, it's a party, so let them be.

Other things to consider are how much to work, how much to commit, and how long your energy lasts during the trip. You actually need to gauge it based on what you know about your boss, or better said, the parents. You'll learn that they're all different when it comes to spending time with their kids. Some families would love to cook and have breakfast together, so they won't need you until after all that's done and finished. You may be coming to their room around 8:30 am or 9 am, so you don't have to be up so early. And you may be helping until dinner and be dismissed by then because there are parents who love bathing their children all by themselves, so this schedule even for the trip is pretty amazing. My advice to you is to work hard and think about it in a sense that you're working 8 to 10 hours and it's not too tiring.

But some other families will need you to be there a lot earlier because of their lifestyle, maybe they go out every night or whatever other reasons so they're tired in the mornings and will need you there at 7 am to feed the child breakfast, work the whole day, feed the child dinner and bathe the child.

So at this point, if you're traveling, you kind of know the parents' approach towards the children. And you have options based on that. For the parents who are hands-on with their children, I'd commit every day to doing the same thing during the trip.

For families who you know will you have to work all day, during the trip I'd still be all in. However, if it's a trip of two weeks or more, I'd definitely ask or talk about days off and a schedule. When you get too tired, you don't think straight, you start criticizing the family, you don't want to go to work, and so on. Talk about it with the parents. Explain that you need to be rested in order to properly care for the child. I always recommend talking to the parents about everything. Communication is key to keeping harmony flowing.

After the trip is over and you're back home, you will realize that you worked a lot and that it was a little fun but a lot harder than usual. And while talking about it with your family and friends, there will always be someone asking, "And what did they give you?" "Did you get something extra?" "Did they pay you overtime?"

The truth is, as long as they pay you what you agreed on and you're satisfied, don't let anyone fill up your head with ideas. Every family is different. They have no obligation to give anything "extra" unless their hearts want to.

I've had families who will be grateful and express their gratitude verbally, and I've had families that send small gifts to my daughter every Christmas even long after I was gone.

So keep on working faithfully without expecting the "extras." This way, there won't be disappointments and if the "extras" come, they will be a nice surprise!

CHAPTER 15

FINISHING WITH THE FAMILY: LEAVING A LEGACY

Before I start this chapter, I want to say that my idea of being a nanny is to help as many families as I can, in the sense that I've never worked for a family for more than three years. After three years, you're ready to move along to another child. Why only three years? Because as I said from the beginning, I like to start with new parents with their first born, and give them a head start for their future children. I know how difficult it is for new parents to figure out how to take care of their new baby, so I would always choose an infant to walk her through her first years of life. In LA, when the child turns three years old she most likely starts preschool, if not before. I love the idea of being able to help when people most need it. I like the feeling that I'm making an impact and the idea that I will leave a legacy. After the first child, families know better with their second.

Without knowing and because of my training, I became an early childhood educator, an infant care specialist.

During the interview, I would explain this. I would let the parents know how crucial the first five years are. 80% of the brain develops during the first three years, and 90% percent until 5 years (Reef 2012). So the way we care for and engage the baby becomes of great importance. I would explain to the parents how the Educaring® Approach will help. After this conversation, the parents generally would agree with me;

during this conversation, I also discuss how I finished with the previous family and that if I would've stayed with my last family longer than three years, we wouldn't be having our conversation. By the end of my third year, the parents I helped completely understood these ideas because of the resulting effects in their children. Every child after my three years of service was so ready to go ahead with their little lives, at school and with the new nanny who at this point, will find a confident, secure child who knows what's going on and understands her surroundings. Now, that doesn't mean that it's easy. Moving along is hard. It's hard for the child you're leaving and it's hard for the nanny.

Six months before closing my three years I'd remind the parents about it so they can start thinking about hiring the new nanny for the child. Ten weeks before finishing, I'd start talking to the child about it very casually. I'd say, "Rosie is a big girl now. Very soon Rosie will be going to preschool." Once while drawing during my daily routine with a child I cared for, he asked, "Can you draw a mermaid for me?" and I'd said, "Sure. Would you like to help?" even when he just scribble scrabbles. After we finished the drawing he just tore it apart and I saw that as my chance to talk about me leaving soon, by saying something like, "When you're at preschool, you aren't going to be able to rip it out and you also won't be allowed to scribble scrabble on your friends' papers, you know." Always bring up what will be happening to the child's attention.

Little by little, without creating drama or stress, the child will be ready for the big change. Once they've found their new nanny, I'd suggest a three-week transitioning time to the parents. The first week, the new nanny will be an observer and I'll show her the child's routine and how I engage her by modeling. The second week, the new nanny will be in action and I'll be the observer; whenever necessary, like when the child comes to me I'd explain that X will be helping with lunch today or that X will help her pick shoes. One other important thing here is that whenever I get to meet the new nanny, as soon as I see him/her with the child present, I'd greet the new nanny very warmly, as if we've known each other for a long time. I'll give the new nanny a hug, when the child sees that, she thinks, "My nanny, the one I trust with my life, is hugging X," and this works wonders. The child feels a little familiarized with the new nanny because of that.

During the third week, I'm on and off and then I go. Usually, the families I worked for would throw a little goodbye party in the kitchen or plan a nice dinner out with the children and that's great. Hopefully, you'll get one of those. It's important here that you maintain a cheerful attitude and positive, happy face. Not to say that you're pretending, but if you used or follow the basic principles of the Educaring® Approach, by the end of your service you'll feel accomplished. When people have asked me, "How can you not be sad? It's so sad," and my answer always is because I know what I gave to this child every minute of those three years; I feel that I gave it all. I gave my best and I didn't keep anything. The child knows that and God knows that. In my experience, going through this transition, the child would be ready and better prepared for the big change than the parents. Every time I had to leave, the parents were the ones who struggled the most.

Then I'll suggest a visiting plan. I'd come back for the first visit after two weeks of my departure, then after four weeks, and finally after six weeks. Then I'll visit whenever I'm invited. I suggest this because it's by the third week that the child would sink into the change that just happened and will start asking for you. During my first visit, again with a very happy face, I'll show up at the door and greet the child and the new nanny very warmly, and start asking how things are going in a positive way. "I've heard you guys are having so much fun together," and if the child says, "I miss you," I'll say, "I miss you too," always acknowledging the child's feelings. It's ok to miss people you love! This visiting plan is very important to teach the child that people who were close to her didn't just disappear and then they always move along in a healthy way. At least, that's what I've seen in my experience.

Upon leaving, I would bring small presents for the children, maybe some drawings or art we created together. The greatest thing I'll bring is a photo album with unofficial photos I took during the course of the three years, funny silly pictures and videos from when I took them to gym classes or cute play dates with their friends. Parents love and appreciate that.

I have to mention that every three years that I was able to find a new family with a newborn gave me the chance to gain more and more experience and raise my income. I basically had a raise every three years, due to the amazing references and recommendation letters the families I helped.

Nevertheless, it's always up to you to stay longer. You don't have to finish after three years if you feel like you love the family and it's too hard for you to leave the child, don't do it. This book is a guide for a nanny who desires to work in LA, is interested in early childhood education, likes to help new families, and have a fresh start every three years. Three years is a long time, believe me.

Lastly I have to say that working in LA all these years has been rewarding and exciting. You never know who your next employer could be, actors, actresses, musicians, CAA agents, artists, models, writers. I've worked for all of them, I learned from them, they were always all good to me and to my daughter.

Thank you so much for reading this book and I wish you the best in your career as a nanny. And parents, good luck in your search for the next caregiver of your children, you know now how crucial are their first five years! Choose wisely.

SOME OF THE CHILDREN I
SHARED MY LIFE WITH

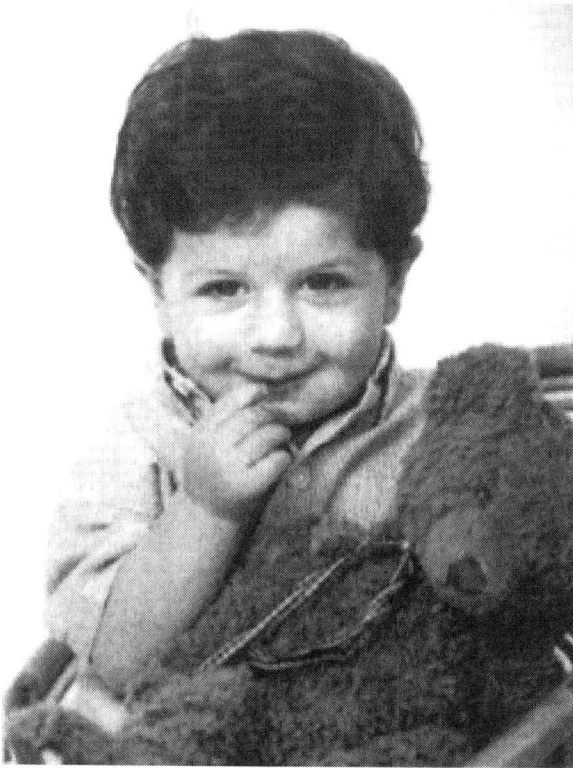

Max

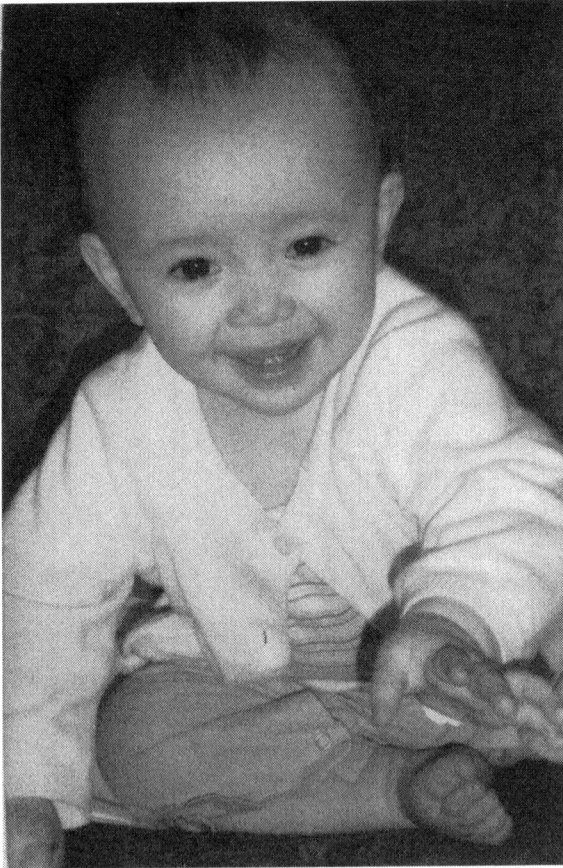

Aislinn

Naya

Yara and Sayeed

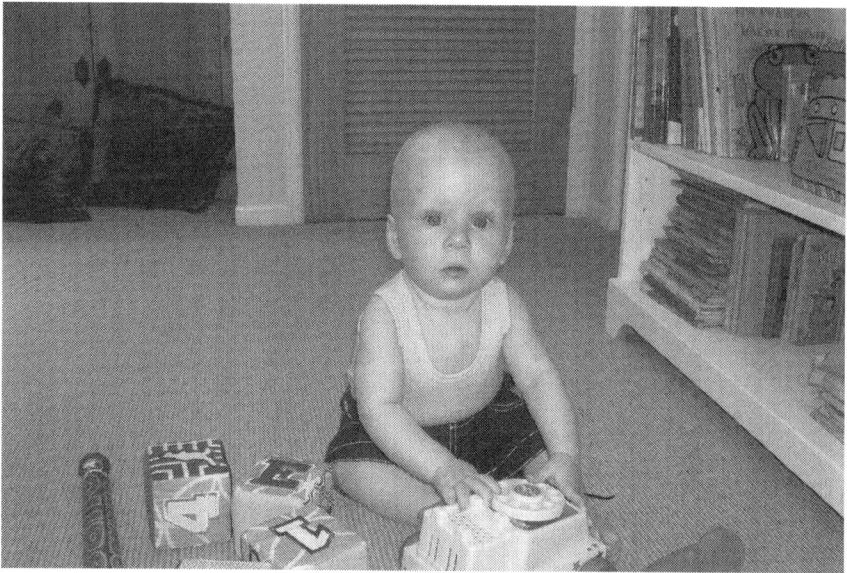

Owen

RESOURCES

Childcare is a broad subject. Keep yourself up to date! Here are some wonderful resources for you to continue learning and understanding the Educaring® Approach

RIE® and Magda Gerber's Educaring® Approach

The RIE® website includes information on RIE® membership and classes for parents and professionals, as well as a selection of books, DVDs, and audio recordings for purchase. http://www.rie.org/

RIE® Parent-Infant Guidance Classes
http://www.rie.org/classes/parent-infant

RIE® Professional Development Classes
http://www.rie.org/classes/profdevel

Resources for Purchase
http://www.rie.org/store

Online Parenting Websites

Magda Gerber
        http://www.magdagerber.org/
Elevating Childcare
        http://www.janetlansbury.com/
Lisa Sunbury
        http://www.regardingbaby.org/

Little Learners Lodge
  http://mmpschool.com/
Conscious Parenting Guide
  http://www.consciousparentingguide.com
Emily Plank
  http://abundantlifechildren.com
Nursery World
  http://www.nurseryworld.co.uk

Nursing

http://thebabybond.com/ComfortNursing.html

Recipes

Super Baby Food (1998) by Ruth Yaron

Vegetarian Mother's Cookbook (2005) by Cathe Olson

Places that allow you to post your ad

Gymboree
Jag's Gym
The Pump Station
Los Angeles Public Library

Other Resources
City Baby L.A. (2011) by Linda Meadow and Lisa Rocchio

Swimming Lessons: Jessie Sheldon (310) 428 8262
Jessie is the gentlest swimming teacher I've ever met, RIE inspired.

WORKS CITED

Child care industry statistics. (2012). Retrieved from http://www. primroseschools.com/sites/all/themes/primroseschools/ files/press-kit-child-care-statistics.pdf

Educaring® Approach. (2012). Retrieved from http://www.rie. org/educaring

Gerber, M. (2003). *Dear parent: Caring for infants with respect.* (2nd Edition ed.). Los Angeles, California: Resources for Infant Educarers® (RIE®).

Gerber, M. (1984). Dear magda, dear parent. *Educaring, 5*(1).

Gerber, M. (2000). *Rie® manual for parents and professionals.* (10th ed.). Los Angeles, California: Resources for Infant Educarers® (RIE®).

Gerber, M. (2012). *Your self-confident baby: How to encourage your child's natural abilities from the very beginning.* Wiley.

Gerber, M., Greenwald, D., & Weaver, J. (2013). *The rie® manual expanded edition.* (p. 228). Los Angeles, California: Resources for Infant Educarers® (RIE®).

Gerber, M., Owen, S., & Petrie, S. (2005). *Authentic relationships in group care for infants and toddlers resources for infant educarers (rie) principles into practice.* Los Angeles, California: Resources for Infant Educarers® (RIE®).

In memoriam. (2012). Retrieved from http://www.magdagerber.org/in- memoriam.html

Lansbury, J. (2011, August 12). [Weblog message]. Retrieved from http://www.janetlansbury.com/2011/08/dealing-with-diaper-changing-disasters/

Piccalo, G. (2010, October 31). The secret celebrity parenting craze. *The Daily Beast.* Retrieved from http://www.thedailybeast.com/articles/2010/10/31/rie-the-celebrity-parenting-craze.html

Relationship—the pikler collection. (2011). Retrieved from http://thepiklercollection.weebly.com/relationship.html

Reef, G. (2012, October 13). [Web log message]. Retrieved from http://policyblog.usa.childcareaware.org/2012/10/13/child-care-training-matters-2/

Selver, C. (1994). Foreword. *Sensory Awareness Foundation Bulletin*, (14), 1.

Weissbluth, M. (1999). *Healthy sleep habits, happy child.* Ballatine Books.

I hope you enjoyed this book. If you would like to leave
a comment or ask a question you can write to:

theLAnannybook@hotmail.com
or
Facebook: The LA Nanny Book
Twitter: @thelananny

Printed in Great Britain
by Amazon